Cyber Defense
for
Law Enforcement
and
First Responders

Easy to Follow Step-by-Step
Recommendations

CECILIA ANASTOS

ISBN-13: 9798343683707

Cover design by: ViknCharlie at Fiverr.com
Library of Congress Control Number: 1-14368073581
Printed in the United States of America

DEDICATION

To my dearest friends FBI Special Agent (Ret.) Anthony Montgomery, SDPD Capt. (Ret.) Jorge Duran, Detective Nick Selby and Detective (Ret.) Cory W. Scott

.

CONTENTS

Preface

In the early XXI century, I was known as the "queen of OSINT[1]." I figured out how to find anybody who had left a digital footprint. I put Johnny Long's techniques[2] on steroids. I developed courses to teach my skills to law enforcement agencies, to the private sector, and to the U.S. Navy SEALs.

One of those courses is about cyber defense. It is about securing your own cyber perimeter and protecting your data. Now, I have adapted the course into a book – the book you are reading. Does reading this book guarantee that you will not be hacked? Nope. Does it guarantee that your credentials (credit card numbers and Internet passwords) held by third parties will be safe? Nope. Does it guarantee you will never lose your data? Nope.

But it guarantees that you will not be the first target a hacker will select, and it will teach you what to do in the event your credentials and/or data are stolen due to your cyber negligence or the cyber negligence of others.

Because criminals, in particular those associated with human trafficking and drug cartels, have often better penetration technology than the Federal, State, Local and Tribal departments in charge of pursuing them, when you harden your cyber perimeter, you are also protecting your family. Most of you carry your personal devices, and in fact, you use them to search things related to your cases. These criminals can easily find out where you and your loved one live.

Technology is constantly changing. So is the modus operandi of criminals. Cyber criminals take advantage of Internet users' lack of attention to online security. And you might be surprised at how many people fail to have adequate online security in place.

Therefore, this is not a book that will *give* you "the fish" but a book that will *teach* you "how to fish." You will learn how to configure any new device, even if the user interface for that device is not described in this book. You will

---

[1] Open-Source Information Intelligence (OSINT)

[2] Johnny Long is a white hat hacker who in 2005 published a book titled Google Hacking for Penetration Testers.

learn behavioral techniques that should help you safeguard your cyber perimeter regardless of the passage of time.

You might wonder why I have not talked about The Onion Ring (TOR), and the Dark Web. This is not a book about collecting open-source information. This is a book about hardening your personal cyber perimeter.

Although I mentioned many services and products in this book, none of them are sponsoring me. These are products that I have used for a long time, and I find them to be reliable and trustworthy.

Some of you might find these recommendations easy to follow on your own. Others might need additional help. If you would like to receive additional assistance from me via video conference, book an appointment at my website www.anastosresearch.com. I can answer your questions in detail, solve a particular problem you might have or guide to additional resources that you might need in order to solve your problem.

You did an important thing by picking up this book. Making your digital safety a priority is something you will never regret.

CHAPTER 1 - PASSWORDS

In this chapter, I will present you with two ways of creating and managing your passwords for all your online accounts. One method is using the for-pay services of 1Password or BitWarden. The other method is the "old-fashioned way," where you do not depend on a third party to create and manage your passwords but create and manage them yourself.

Many individuals are afraid of not remembering their passwords. Passwords is the topic of jokes about people putting their passwords on a paper under the keyboard, and silly passwords like 1234password. A password is the one thing that when stolen will cause havoc in your privacy and finances.

Regardless of the method you choose, both sides of the aisle agree that you do not need to change your password every 90 days. Once you create a strong password, there is no need to change it unless you receive a notification from the service provider that your password has been stolen.

Password Managers

There are many companies that offer password management services. Some have already been hacked several times. The three I list below are, as of today, managing their cybersecurity with state-of-the-art technology, and a leadership that understands the importance of cybersecurity.

1Password

1Password (https://1password.com/) promises you to protect all your sign-ins in a secure vault which in turn allows you to securely share those passwords with family, if needed. You can also sign in to all your services from any device. Moreover, 1Password allows you to manage the permissions you have granted to ensure that only devices that are not infected with malware can have access.

This company offers individual, family and business plans. The individual plan at the time of writing this book is $3.99 per month or $2.99 if you pay annually. The family plan is $6.95 or $4.99 if you pay annually.

BitWarden

BitWarden (https://bitwarden.com/) is an open-source password manager that offers individuals and business plans. Your data is stored in a vault that has end-to-end encryption[3]. It is in the cloud and it will only transmit via secure channels. Should any of the passwords you use be compromised, Bitwarden will alert you about it.

The individual plan runs for $4 per month billed annually only.

IronVest

IronVest, formerly Blur, - https://ironvest.com[4] offers many services. (See Figure 1 - IronVest to Store Non-Critical Passwords.) We will explore some of these services through the book. In this section, I want to bring your attention to IronVest's **Access Guard** feature.

Once you create an account with IronVest, and download the extension to your browsers (Safari or Google), you can open the **Access Guard** feature. Click on **Access** Guard and select **Logins & Passwords**. Each time you log into an account, IronVest will ask you whether you want or do not want to save that password with them. I recommend you say yes for all accounts, except for your critical accounts such as financial institutions, medical services, Dropbox, and your email. By saving your login and password, IronVest automatically fills in that information whenever you access the

---

[3] End-to-end Encryption is a security method where your data is encrypted in your device and can only be decrypted on the device of the person receiving that data. The data is not stored in a server. The only people who can read that data are you, the sender, and the person who receives your message.

[4] I do not receive compensation from any of the services I recommend. I only recommend services that I have used for a long time and have proven to me to be safe.

website in question.

Most of the services provided by IronVest are free of charge. I only use **Access Guard**, **Privacy**, and **Tracking.**

Figure 1 - IronVest to Store Non-Critical Passwords

Creating and Managing your Own Passwords

According to the National Institute of Science and Technology (NIST), you need to use a password with a minimum length of eight characters. This works for accounts where you do not store critical information such as newspapers, blogs, podcasts, etc. For the accounts that contain critical information such as your finances, email and health records, I recommend a minimum of 12 characters. Although, in my opinion, the ideal length is a 16-character password.

Your password must have upper- and lower-case letters, numbers, and a special character from this selection: !@$& or space bar.

How to come up with an easy to remember password?

For using numbers, I like to replace the vowels with numbers:

A=4   E=3   I=1   O=0

You can also replace the letter L with the number 7.

Then, I select a phrase or the full name of someone important to me. For this example, I will build a password using my name: Cecilia Anastos

!C3c1714 4n4$t0$ = 16-character password (Notice the space between the two number 4s in the middle)

I have replaced the vowels and the letter L in my first name with numbers,

3

and the letter S in my last name with the symbol $. Therefore, I have a password with upper and lower case, numbers and symbols.

You SHOULD NOT recycle passwords; in other words, you cannot use the same password in multiple accounts that contain critical information. When the hackers steal the passwords of one service, that password will be useless in all your other services because you have not recycled your passwords. Studies show that 50-65% of people recycle passwords across multiple online accounts. This is a serious security concern. For example, you cannot use the password you use to log into your bank account to log into a social media account, or your health records, etc. Because when you use a unique password per account, and that password gets stolen, then it is useful in only one account versus giving the hacker access to all of your accounts.

Let's assume that the password I created above is for my email account. In that case, I should create a different password for my bank account. Don't let the idea of creating multiple passwords be daunting though. **You only need to change one character in your password to create a new fingerprint and make it completely different.**

$C3c1l14 4n4$t0$ - Notice that I have changed the first character of my original password. I added a dollar symbol instead of the exclamation mark. This now becomes a new password for my bank account.

Where do you store passwords?

For the password that you manually create and manage, you can store them in a spreadsheet or Notes. In that spreadsheet or note, you write a hint of your password. (See Figure 2– Spreadsheet Sample with hints). DO NOT write the password down because should anyone access that document, that person will not be able to see the written passwords. This is your layer of security. Only you know what the hint means. You only need to write a hint such as:

!Name$ - Email

$Name$ = bank

SERVICE	HINT
Gmail	!FavMovie! No spaces
DropBox	&FavoriteMovie!
Credit Card	$FavoriteMovie!
Bank Account	$FavoriteMovie$

Figure 2– Spreadsheet Sample with hints

Two-Factor Authentication

Passwords alone are not enough to secure your accounts because passwords can be stolen regardless of the method you use to store them. You need to use a two-factor authentication (also known as two-step authentication), such as a text, email, or an authentication app such as the one created by Google. See the CHAPTER 7 - TWO-FACTOR AUTHENTICATION.

Knowing what you know now about passwords, take some time in the next week to re-visit all of your passwords and ask yourself whether they are secure. If you do not already have a spreadsheet such as what I suggest above, create one.

CHAPTER 2 – HACKING AND YOUR CYBER BEHAVIOR

Passwords are one way to protect your data, but the devices you use to access that data must be secured as well. If a hacker plants a Trojan horse in your computer or phone, that hacker can see everything you do on your device, including entering your passwords.

The following is just a partial list of what a hacker can do once inside your device:

- Find out all system information, including hardware being used and the exact version of your operating system, including security patches.

- Control all the processes currently running on your system.

- View and modify your registry.

- Modify your host file.

- **Control your computer, mobile devices, and security cameras from a remote location.**

- Execute various types of scripts on your system.

- Put files in your system.

In simple words, you no longer own your device. The hacker does.

I have heard too many times excuses such as "this computer does not have anything important," "I do not care if someone hacks it, there is nothing of value to me," and "it is my kids' computer/phone/tablet." Every single electronic device can be compared to a hammer. In our daily life, we can use a hammer to do good such as building a house or to commit a crime such a breaking a person's skull. The same principle applies to electronic devices. They can be used for something good or to commit a crime. Your electronic devices, regardless of their content or who uses them, could become an instrument of a crime in the hands of a hacker.

A hacker can take control of your kid's tablet and use it to commit cybercrimes.

> **Side Story**: About 10 years ago, while I was still teaching my Cyber Defense class to the U.S. Navy SEALs, I got a call from a previous student telling me that the security cameras in his house were no longer under his control. Someone else was turning them on and off at will. I drove to his house, and began looking at one device at time. I asked for the kid's Android tablet, and bingo! It had been hacked to the wazoo. From that innocent tablet, the hacker was watching my previous student and his family, day and night.

After you read this book once, and secure your own personal devices, you need to follow through with all the other devices in your household. The security measures that I teach here will not preclude any member of your family to have fun with technology. It will just keep prying eyes outside of your home perimeter.

The graphic on Figure 3- Internet Usage by Nation (2024) shows that the United States is not the country with most Internet connections, yet it is the country most hacked according to a study conducted by BlackBerry[5] titled Global Threat Intelligence Report[6]. (See Figure 4 - Most hacked countries as of 2023)

---

[5] Blackberry, even though its smartphone became obsolete, remains a relevant company because of its transitioning to a leading cybersecurity company who now specializes in software solutions for the Internet of Things (IoT) within the automotive industry.

[6] https://www.blackberry.com/us/en/solutions/threat-intelligence/2023/threat-intelligence-report-jan

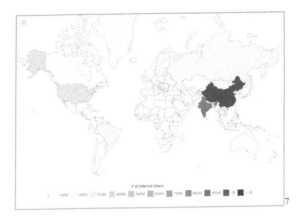

Figure 3- Internet Usage by Nation (2024)

Hackers go after US citizens mainly because of our power of acquisition. We have more money than others. There are some who hack because of political motivations such as state sponsored hackers and terrorists. We can divide hackers in five categories:

1. Recreational: This hacker looks for fame and notoriety. This person uses known exploits and has limited technical resources.
2. Criminal: Although this hacker has limited technical capabilities, vandalism is the preferred choice of damage.
3. Hacktivist: This relentless hacker is emotionally motivated to make a statement using targeted attacked. The hacker has access to vast networks. The most famous hacktivist group is Anonymous.
4. Organized crime: Some hackers and hacking groups work to obtain financial gains. Nigerian hackers and the Eurasian Mafia are known to earn billions of dollars from hacking activities. These groups have significant technical resources and capabilities with well-established syndicates, and technology such as adware, crimeware, IP theft, etc.
5. State sponsored: China, Russia, North Korea and Iran are at the forefront of countries engaged in state-sponsored hacking. These countries engage in cyberwar to steal state and industrial secrets. They are highly sophisticated with unlimited resources and present a persistent threat not only to our national security but to the well-being of citizens as well. For example, a state sponsored attack could

---

[7] Source: https://worldpopulationreview.com/country-rankings/internet-users-by-country

target a hospital to seed chaos in our population.

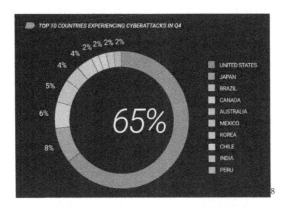

Figure 4 - Most hacked countries as of 2023

Cybercrime is the use of a technology device (computer, smartphone, tablet, external hard drive, etc.) to commit illegal activities such as identity theft, stealing intellectual property, transmitting child pornography images, stalking, and overwhelming a website with traffic to slow it down.

Along the following pages, you will find references to different types of cybercrimes such as *phishing and its variations* (someone sending you a text, email or calling you to extract information from you or to trick you into clicking a URL link that will put malware in your device); Internet of Things (IoT) (devices that listen to your conversations such as Alexa and other sensors placed in your home/office); and malicious applications that hackers manage to introduce in Apple Store and Google Play in spite of the efforts of these companies to prevent that.

As of March 2024, Google Play reported that 90 malicious Android apps had been downloaded 5.5 million times.[9]

Behavior in Cyber Defense
The hardening of your electronic devices is one component of protecting you against hackers. Your behavior toward cyber defense; i.e., the discipline you

---

[8] https://blogs.blackberry.com/content/dam/blogs-blackberry-com/images/blogs/2023/02/top-10-countries-attacked-by-malware.png

[9] https://www.bleepingcomputer.com/news/security/over-90-malicious-android-apps-with-55m-installs-found-on-google-play/ accessed on 6 August 2024

instill in yourself when you are accessing the Internet, is also a paramount step in keeping you safe from hackers.

Because of the work you do, this cyber defense behavior has to be practiced by all members of your household. You can have the most secure cyber perimeter, and one of your kids brings a friend with an infected device, and your kid (against your instructions) shares the Wi-Fi password with the friend. There goes the privacy and security of the whole family. See Configuring your Wi-Fi.

I am aware that I am asking to change things on your behavior when handling technology that might make you and your family members roll your eyes. Smartphones have created an impulsive brain that controls the finger you use to click on things. You need to slow down, and be present in the moment when you are handling technology. You cannot do the look and touch effect anymore. You must look, analyze, deploy your knowledge of cyber defense, and act upon the information you received accordingly. If you need help to learn how to slow down your brain to be in the present moment, and process information without rushing, I recommend reading Crawford Coates's *Mindful Responder* (https://amzn.to/3Minq13)

Figure 5 - Behavior and Cyber Defense shows a scenario that could happen at your home or your office. Inside the wall, you have multiple individuals connected to an Internet service provider that allows Internet access via a direct connection to the modem, or through Wi-Fi or cellular (3G, 4G, 5G).

On the perimeter wall shown in Figure 5, these providers use tools such firewalls, passwords, intrusion detection systems (IDS), and many other state-of-the-art tools that if they truly worked 100% of the time, we would not be reading about major hacking attacks. On your own devices, you have also access to certain tools that prevent non-authorized individuals to access your devices: passwords, firewalls, encryption, and anti-virus software.

In spite of all these defense mechanisms, you only need a bad behavior to render all these tools useless. The user of electronic devices is the weakest link in the cyber security chain. For example, recycling passwords (using the same password in multiple important accounts), not locking your cellphone after using it when you are in a public place, not using a Virtual Private Network (VPN) when you access a Wi-Fi. (See CHAPTER 6 - VIRTUAL PRIVATE NETWORKS)

In this book, I put equal emphasis on hardening devices with the assistance of tools as well as on behavior modifications to ensure those tools work in the most effective possible manner.

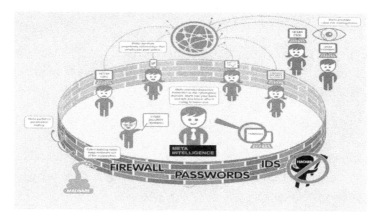

Figure 5 - Behavior and Cyber Defense

URL links and Images

It is possible to be better at your cybersecurity. In most cyber incidents, the weakest link of the cybersecurity chain is the user of technology. It is possible for you to change the way you do things with technology. It is possible for you to change your behavior toward technology.

We all need to be better with our cybersecurity, and that it IS possible. Your first behavior modification habit to incorporate in your routine when working on your computer or mobile device (phone and tablet) is to **stop clicking directly on links**. One of the most prevalent cybercrimes is phishing. A hacker sends you an email or text with a URL link. The email or text looks very much as if it was sent by an organization you trust, such as your banking institution or your email provider. When you click on the link, your device gets infected or you are prompted to enter your credentials into a fake page that looks exactly like the page you want to access. For example, you may receive an email that appears to be from your bank. The email contains instructions with a link to do something. You might click on a link, thinking it will take you to your bank's website. When you click on the link, your device either becomes infected or you are taken to a fake page that looks exactly like your bank's login page. This is how phishing scams achieve their goals of stealing your identity.

Figure 6 - Do Not Click on URL Links shows a smart woman who upon receiving an email with a URL link, she opens a web browser such as Google, DuckDuckGo, Firefox or Safari, and types the name of the website.

Let's explore several potential scenarios, practicing how you can protect yourself by not clicking on URL links.

First Scenario: You receive an email from an organization, including your own department, asking you to click on a link because there is an important message waiting there for you.

Rather than click the link, you will do the following:

- Open a browser of your choice (Google, Safari, DuckDuckGo) and in the search field type the name of the institution the link is supposedly directing you to..
- Click on the institution name to reach its website.
- Select, Log In, or Sign In, and use your usual credentials to sign in.

Once you are inside the real website for that institution, then you can see if the message you received is legit. Let's imagine the message on the email says that there is an important banking message for you. Then, when you log directly to your back account, you can access the message there. If there are none, phone your bank and let them know that you were almost the victim of a phish. The bank will hopefully alert its other customers.

If the email comes from your own workplace, I do not care who sent it (your boss, a colleague), DO NOT click on whatever link or image comes attached on that email, unless you solicited it. Many police departments have been hacked because someone click on an unsolicited image, or a link that arrived via email with a request to complete a form. Before you complete any forms, check with your boss to find out whether it is something the department is sending and it is legit.

Second Scenario: You receive a text message from a friend, inviting you to click on a link to view something.

Rather than click on the link directly in the text message, open a browser of your choice and type in the site address directly. You do not know whether your friends' or family members' devices are safe. It's possible, in this scenario, that your friend's phone was infected with a Trojan virus that is sending texts or emails remotely, unbeknownst to your friend.

For example, at the time of writing this section, the Olympic Games 2024 were taking place in Paris. My friend, Ernie, wanted to show me something on YouTube. He sent me a link via text. I did not click on the link directly. Instead, I went to YouTube and typed the name of the athlete and a portion of the title of the video in YouTube's search bar. I was able to watch what my friend wanted me to see without compromising my devices by clicking on a link that may or may not have been infected.

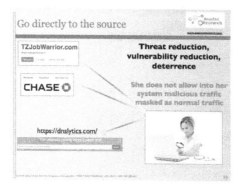

Figure 6 - Do Not Click on URL Links

Look at Figure 6 - Do Not Click on URL Links again. In the lower left, you see a reference to an excellent website that allows you to discover who owns a website. Besides working on the cyber field, I am also a fine art painter. Let's take a look at my website www.ceciliaanastos.com and discover what dnslytics.com tells us about it.

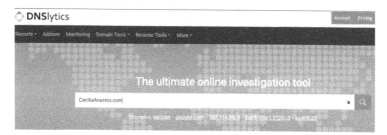

In DNSlytics, you can type in the domain name of any website you want to know more about. The system then provides you with several options. (See Figure 7 - DNSlytics)

My first choice is to go to Option 4 – Domain Report – where you can see who owns the website. Most individuals use a third party to register their websites; therefore, the owner of the website is rarely the name of an individual, but more often a company name, such as Domains by Proxy. Nevertheless, the Domain Report will show you where the website is hosted.

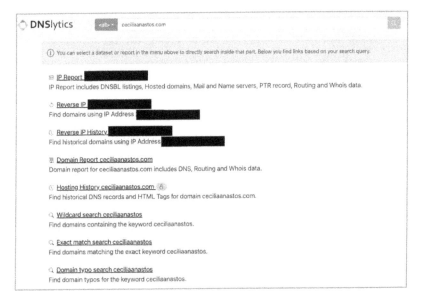

Figure 7 - DNSlytics

On your phone or tablet, touch and hold the URL with your finger carefully, so as to not to click on it but to trigger a dialog box that asks you whether you want to Open, Add to Reading List, or **Copy the URL**. Select **Copy the URL**. Then, open a web browser of your choice. (NOTE: We will talk about best browsers in CHAPTER 9 – SURFING THE WEB UNDETECTED.) Paste the URL into your browser. If the URL has malware, a browser like Google will alert you not to proceed with it. See Figure 8 - Copying a URL on Phone or Tablet, for step-by-step instructions.

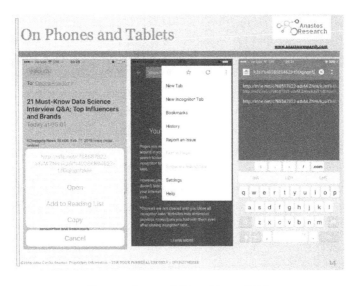

Figure 8 - Copying a URL on Phone or Tablet

Watering Holes

The National Institute of Standards and Technology (NIST) defines a watering hole as infected website which is frequently used by a certain group. The FBI defines watering holes as the computers on the business centers of hotels, the charging stations at airports, rental cars and the advertising pops up that you often see when you are browsing the Internet.

Let's explore in depth solutions to avoid being a victim of a watering hole.

Website Visited by Certain Groups: Let's say that one of your tasks in the company where you work is to purchase goods from a supplier on a regular basis. Most likely, that supplier sends you regular emails with offers or updates regarding an order. A hacker, seeing that you visit and purchase from this supplier's website often, could replicate the site and send you an email with a link to a special offer. If you click on the link and make a purchase, you share your financial information with the hacker.

Solution: In following the recommendation above, DO NOT click on a link received from that supplier. If you receive an email with a discount offer, make a note of the coupon code you are required to use, visit to the supplier's website by entering the URL directly in your browser. You can safely shop from there and enter the coupon code you saw on the email.

If you receive an email that pertains to a specific order, and it says

15

that you need to revise payment, DO NOT click on any link inside the email. Instead, visit the website of the supplier, log in, go to Orders or Order History and you will be able to confirm whether the payment needs to be corrected.

Computers on in hotel business centers at Hotels: In the past, the hotel business center was often used to print boarding passes and send and receive email. These days, the majority of travelers own smartphones/tablets, which have the power of a computer to access the Internet. That means we now use our phones and personal laptops to obtain e-tickets, make payments and send and receive emails. which you can scan at the airport, etc. Nevertheless, should you decide to use a public computer such as one in a hotel business center, be aware that there is a high risk of security compromise. In other words, you need to figure out a way around the need of I do not recommend logging into one any of your valuable accounts (email, bank, etc.) using such public devices. Do you need to print a document? Use your own cellphone or tablet to upload the document to FedEx and they will print it for you.

Charging Stations at Airports: Using a USB charger directly into the charging station is as if you were downloading all of your data into someone's else computer.

Solution: Carry your own charger for your phone/computer/tablet that must be plugged into an electrical outlet. All charging stations at the airport, including those inside the planes and those next to chairs at the gates, have electrical outlets where you can plug in the charging wire for your device.

Rental Cars: DO NOT ever connect your phone via Bluetooth or CarPlay to the rental vehicle, nor use the USB directly on the dashboard. Doing so will download all of your data on the vehicle. This data is then retrieved by the company when you return your vehicle.

Solution: Carry with you a USB connector that plugs into the cigarette lighter of the vehicle. Keep in mind that Android and Apple chargers have slightly different configurations.

CHAPTER 3 – HARDENING DEVICES

Apple products have always been my favorite for security reasons. Because the Android phones have many different user interfaces for the settings screen, I will speak in general terms about what you can do with them to obtain a good level of privacy. As I always say in the classes I teach, if you can ask for a gift during your birthday or Holiday Season, ask for Apple products.

One of the reasons why mobile Apple products are more secure than Android products is that Apple mobile devices come encrypted from factory. You will learn here how to encrypt your Android devices. As long as your phone is locked, the data is encrypted. When you unlock the phone/tablet to use it, you also unencrypt most of the data. This is why it is so important that you keep your mobile devices locked when not directly looking at them.

You will also learn in the following pages how to encrypt your Apple computer hard drive. Then, in the sections **Error! Reference source not found.** and PC Computers, you will learn all about these two other operating systems.

At the end of this Chapter, you will learn how to secure your Wi-Fi router (**Error! Reference source not found.**) which is equivalent to the locks you use in your home.

We will start this chapter by covering the hardening your Apple products, and then I will explain about hardening your Windows and Android products.

Regardless of your choice of brand, when you are and about conducting police or first responder business, I recommend that you place your phone inside a Faraday bag like the ones I recommend in the CHAPTER 8 - TRAVELING. This is particularly important if you work in a high intensity drug trafficking area (HIDTA). While your patrol vehicle is in movement, you can enjoy your personal phone out. When you arrive to the area where you need to leave the car and conduct police/responder business, that phone should be placed inside the Faraday bag.

Apple Smartphones and Tablets

All the settings explained in this section apply equally to the iPhone and iPad. Many also apply to the iWatch. For practical reasons, I will refer to the devices as phone or device.

To reiterate, Apple devices come encrypted from factory, whereas the users must encrypt Android devices. Apple does not allow any anti-virus apps to be downloaded on their phones. If you do a search online, you will find Malwarebytes for the iPhone but this app is not allowed to scan the operating system of the Apple device. When Malwarebytes is installed on an Apple or PC computer, it is allowed to look at the inside of the computer and search for Trojans and other malware. For the iPhone/iPad, you will have to pay a subscription to have an app that it will filter calls (which your service provider usually does and alert you of spam calls), to give you a VPN (I prefer TunnelBear instead and you will learn about it soon), and to block malicious sites when you use Safari but you will turn that function **On** right on your phone (see below). Therefore, there is no need to spend money on this app, or any other app that offers you similar services.

On your Apple device, look for the gray **Settings** square. (See Figure 9. I removed the top portion for security, but your screen should show your photo and name). On the **Settings** screen, touch your name. This brings you to your **Apple ID page,** where you can see your photo and email address associated with the Apple ID. We will navigate each option line-by-line.

Figure 9 - Apple Settings Screen

The first line on the Apple ID page is **Personal Information**. When you click on **Personal Information**, you will see your name and birthday fields. Below, it says **Communication Preferences**. Click on it and gray out all the three options. By doing this, you ensure that you will not receive emails with links that pose a serious risk to your cyber security. If you want to learn about all new Apple features, visit Apple's website at www.Apple.com, rather than clicking on links you are emailed about Apple products. By doing this, you can see all there is to see about Apple products, without endangering your cyber perimeter.

Let's go back one screen by clicking on the **Back** button that you see on the upper left corner of your phone or tablet. Click on **Apple ID** located on the upper left corner to go back to the **Apple ID page**.

From the **Apple ID** page, select the second line – **Sign-in & Security,** Figure 10. On that page, you can see the email address associated with your Apple ID, and any other email address you desire to share. Below your email and phone numbers, you will see the blue title **Change Password**. Click on **Two-**

Factor Authentication and turn it on by adding your phone number. The **Security Keys** line will give you the option to use Security Keys provided by a third-party hardware provider. I prefer to use verification codes because I do not trust third party providers. Let's go back one screen to the **Sign-in & Security**.

Figure 10 - Sign-In & Security

Click on **Sign in with Apple**, and you will see all the apps in your device that are using your Apple ID to sign in. Take a careful look at that list, and delete the apps you have stopped using. Also delete any apps for which you no longer desire to use your Apple ID to sign in. The less you expose your Apple ID, the better.

Select **Account Recovery** to set up a trusted person who can assist you in recovering access to your account should you happen to forget your password.

Select **Legacy Contact** to choose the person whom you want to have access to all of your information after your death. If that person is in your Apple address book, their name and contact information is easy to import. If the person is not in your Apple contacts, first add the person to your contacts and then go back to Legacy Contact and list the info there. By listing a Legacy Contact, you will allow that contact to have access to all devices that use the

Apple ID, such as iPhones, iPads, iWatches and Mac computers.

The last option on the **Apple ID page** is **Automatic Verification**. (See Figure 10.)

On the upper left corner of your phone, touch the blue title, **Apple ID**, to go back to the Apple ID page where you again see your photo and email address at the top of the page.

The third title on the **Apple ID page** is **Payment & Shipping**. Click on that and enter your Apple ID password. This required password is not what you use to unlock the phone. It is your Apple ID password that you use when you make purchases on the Apple Store.

On this page, you can enter a credit card that you want to use for purchases you make with your device. I recommend using a credit card with a limited low maximum available amount, and that you monitor the card activity monthly, in case it is compromised and you see charges that are not yours. Although it is quite convenient to have a credit card stored in your phone, as well as having automatic renewals on a credit card, these are often stolen. A few days before the Holiday Season of 2024, 5 million credit card numbers were stolen and leaked online.[10]

You can also add money to your Apple account, and add other payment methods. I leave this up to your preferences. Follow Apple instructions on how to add payment methods to your Apple account and wallet.

At the bottom of this screen, you have the option to enter the shipping address where you want to receive your goods from purchases made at the Apple Store.

On the upper left corner, touch the blue title, **Apple ID**. On this page, select **Subscriptions**. You will see all the services to which you are subscribed with your Apple ID and the credit card you have on file with each of those subscriptions, such as newspapers and any app that requires an annual or monthly payment. This is the page where you can also cancel any subscription you no longer want. Touch again the **Apple ID** blue button on the upper left

---

[10] https://www.malwarebytes.com/blog/news/2024/12/5-million-payment-card-details-stolen-in-painful-reminder-to-monitor-christmas-spending accessed on 23 Dec 2024

corner to return to the main Apple ID page.

On the **Apple ID** page, click on **iCloud.** Before touching any of the settings on this page, It is important to know that the Apple iCloud is not a secure environment or, at least, not as secure as Apple tries to convince you that it is. Do you want proof? Ask Hollywood star Jennifer Lawrence how she feels now that all of her personal and intimate photos that were stored in her iCloud are floating freely all over the Internet. Later in the book, we will talk about the best online storage service. (See CHAPTER 5 – ENCRYPTED STORAGE.)

On the **iCloud** page, select **Manage Account Storage** and **DO NOT** select **Share with Family**. You want your devices to be compartmentalized. If you opt to **"Share with Family,"** then all devices that are connected to that link are susceptible to compromise, even if only one device on the platform is the compromise target. Each device has its own Apple ID, i.e.; each family member has their own Apple ID. By not selecting **Share with Family,** if one device gets compromised by hackers or thieves, all the other devices remain relatively safe.

Also on the iCloud page, you will see a **Recommended for You** title. I recommend you ignore this feature, because the fewer features you have on the iCloud, the safer you are.

Now, locate the section, **APPS USING iCLOUD.** Turn all those options **OFF**. Notice that at the end of the list, there is the **Show More** option. When you click on it, you will see the full list of Apps using iCloud. I have everything off with the exception of: books, music, and weather.

Now, navigate to the option, **Passwords and Keychain.** Here, you have an option to share your passwords with others. Sharing passwords in the cloud is a major security problem. Therefore, ensure that this option is set to **OFF.**

At the very bottom of the page, select **Look Me Up**. This feature allows other Apple users to find you using the email address that you have used to create an Apple Account. Do you have any apps listed there? Denied them permission to look you up using your Apple ID. This way you can reduce the number of phishing scams you could receive because you reduce the amount of people who has visibility to your email address.

Backing up your phone is an important step in cyber security because should that phone get locked with a ransomware attack, then you will be able to recover all your data from the backup without having to pay the ransom money to the criminals. It is more secure to back up your phone to your computer rather than to the Apple iCloud which is not properly encrypted.

On the upper left corner, click on the blue title **iCloud** to go back to the **iCloud** page. There, select the option that says **iCloud Backup** and turn it **OFF.** Where are you going to back up your phone regularly? You can back up your Apple devices to a Mac or Windows computer. See the detailed explanation below in the section titled, **Error! Reference source not found.** and the section titled, **Error! Reference source not found..**

Now, let's go back to the **Settings** screen on your Apple device (iPhone, iPad, etc.). Click on the line that contains your photo to enter the **Apple ID** page again. Then, click on the **iCloud** option. Scroll down until you see the part of the screen shown in **Figure 11 - iCloud Screen.**

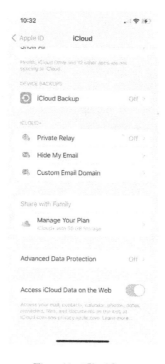

Figure 11 - iCloud Screen

On the **iCloud** screen, look for the **Private Relay** and turn it **On**. You will be re-directed to the **Private Relay** screen. Here you will be given the option to hide your IP address[11] and browsing activity in Safari (the official Internet browser for Apple devices). It will also protect your unencrypted internet traffic so no one can see who you are and the websites you are visiting, in case you forgot to have your VPN on.

Then, click on **IP Address Location** and select **Maintain general location**. The other option Apple gives you here is to use country and time zone. However, it is best when you do not disclose the country and time zone you are in. The more privacy you grant to yourself, the saver you will be online. On the upper left corner of the screen, click the blue title **Back** to return to the **Private Relay** screen. Look again at the upper left corner of the screen, and touch the blue title **iCloud** to return to the **iCloud** page.

On the **iCloud** page, select **Hide My Email.** On this page, you are giving the choice to **Create New Address**. This allows you to create an email address which domain will read @privaterelay.appleid.com. For example, it could be noname22@ privaterelay.appleid.com.

Let's say that you want to register to any of the apps that deliver restaurant food to your home. Instead of using your real email address, you create a random email address using **Create New Address.** If the food app company gets hacked, all the email addresses the company has are exposed. When you protect your real email address by using the **Hide My Email** feature and create a new email address with the **Create New Address** feature, your real email address will be protected.

The **Hide My Email** and **Create New Address** features are also useful when subscribing to a magazine or service that periodically sends you emails and you do not want that service to have your real email address. By clicking on the **Create New Address** you will be able to create a random email address that will forward automatically to the email connected to your Apple ID.

Later on the book, you will learn about another way to mask your email

---

[11] The Internet Protocol (IP) Address is a unique set of characters that identifies each device (computer, phone, Internet modem and router). This is a unique address, like a fingerprint. It is something that you want to protect.

address, in the section Masked Email Addresses.

On the upper left corner of your screen, let's touch the blue title **iCloud** to return to the **iCloud** page. On the option **Custom Email Domain**, click and read what Apple has to offer for you there. You can decide whether you want to utilize this service.

Now, let's move to the **Advanced Data Protection** option. Click on **Advanced Data Protection** to turn it **ON.** Earlier I recommended against using the iCloud as a storage. However, if you already *are* using iCloud for storage, Advanced Data Protection will ensure that whatever you have on the iCloud gets covered with end-to-end encryption. This means that the data will be readable only when you use your trusted devices to access it.

To utilize this service, from the **Advanced Data Protection option,** at the bottom of the screen, touch the blue title, **Turn On Advanced Data Protection**. A new screen pops up. At the bottom of the screen, touch, **Set Up Account Recovery**. There, you will be able to select a recovery contact and key. Follow the screen instructions to complete the process. Then, return to the **iCloud** page.

At the bottom of the **iCloud** page, turn on the option, **Access iCloud Data on the Web** so you can log into the cloud using your computer. **DO NOT** use a public computer to log into the cloud. Ensure you are using your own Wi-Fi and that you have a VPN on. We will talk more about all this in later sections of the book.

Now, touch on the blue title, **Apple ID** on the upper left corner of your device to return to the **Apple ID** page one more time.

Look for the title, **Media & Purchases**. Click and you will see a popup window appear. The window will come from the bottom of the device with the option to **Sign Out** from of the Apple Store, **Password Settings** to change your password, or **View Account** to take a look at your Apple Store account.

We are now again at the **Apple ID** page looking at **Find My**. Click on **Find My** and then on the option, **Find My iPhone.** Turn this option **OFF.** Yes, you read that correctly. The **Find my iPhone** option is one of the biggest security holes for electronic devices. If you can find your phone, so can the hackers.

If you are concerned about misplacing your phone, I suggest you buy this amazing phone case and holder with a clip made by Aduro[12]. The clip allows you to attach your phone to your clothing. When I wear a dress, I attach the clip to the neckline of the dress.

Aduro Combo Case & Holster.

Another security threat with the **Find My** feature is that the device's location service must be constantly on. As you will learn and hopefully implement, your location services should always off, except when you are using a navigator.

Let's go back to the **Apple ID** page.

You will see the list of all the devices using your Apple ID. I recommend that you monitor this frequently.

---

[12] I buy mine at Amazon.com

The **Contact Verification** option I leave to your discretion. We will use more secure options for texting than the message app that comes with your phone by default. Keep in mind that Apple Message uses end-to-end encryption by design, so your messages cannot be read while traveling from one device to the next.

If you ever want to sign out from the Apple ID, you will find this option at the very end of the **Apple ID** page.

From the upper left corner of your screen, let's touch the blue title **Settings**, as shown in Figure 9 - Apple Settings Screen.

Click on the **Wi-Fi** page. You will see that it is turned on if green and off if gray. Then, if it is turned on, you can see a list of available Wi-Fi options around your area (100 ft from where you are standing). After the list of **Other Networks**, you see the option **Ask to Join Networks**. Click on that and select the option **Notify.** Let's go back one screen, and now select **Auto-Join Hotspot.** Select the option **Ask to Join.** Go back one more screen, and click the blue title on the upper left corner that says **Settings.**

From the **Settings** page, touch **Bluetooth.** This takes you to the **Bluetooth** page. Bluetooth is the weakest link of any device, in particular, when you are in a public place like a gym, an airport, a restaurant, etc. This is because when the OBEX protocol[13] in the Bluetooth is open to communicate with another device, such as your headphone or car speaker, it does not have nor does it require authentication policies. As a result, a stranger sitting within 10 feet of you could hack your open Bluetooth connection. Therefore, you should turn your Bluetooth **OFF.**[14]

There are several types of Bluetooth hacking:

- Bluebagging: Unauthorized control of your device
- Bluesnarfing: The stealing of email contacts, text messages and/or

---

[13] Object Exchange (OBEX) is a protocol that allows devices to exchange binary objects such as files and business cards over communication channels.

[14] If you wear a lifesaving device such as a glucose monitor, you will not be able to turn your Bluetooth off because these devices communicate via the Bluetooth channel. Be extra aware of text sent to you from numbers you do not recognize, and do not click on any link or photos sent to you via those text messages from unknown parties.

photos by a hacker, using your open Bluetooth connection

- Bluejacking: An unsolicited message from a hacker near you. This is more annoying than dangerous, unless the messages contain a link infected with malware.

- Man-in-the-Middle (or the not-so-fun ménage-à-trois of technology): The interception of all of your communications by a hacker. The hacker can also manipulate your communications by redirecting you to a look-alike page of a website you trust (a bank, for example).

Earlier, I talked about behavior modification. The use of Bluetooth and Location Services are the best examples of your willingness to make a conscious effort to modify behavior. If you want to use the Bluetooth while you are driving, the risk is slightly less than if you are stationary, because it would be harder to catch you and your communication outlets while you are moving. The question is, will you have the mindfulness - in other words, the presence of mind - in the moment of parking your vehicle to think about security measures to protect your cyber perimeter? You might have to begin by placing yellow stickies on the dashboard of your vehicle that read, "Turn BT OFF," and "Turn Location Service OFF," once you reach your destination.

Is this a pain in the rear end? Yes, for some who are used to Bluetoothing their lives off, it could be. But it is no less important than having other protective measures in place in the physical domain to safeguard you. I would love to get out of my car and not have to lock it. But I lock it for my own safety, and I have never regretted that. Turning off your Bluetooth is just one more way to protect yourself and your information.

Why is it so difficult to change cyber behavior? Because a hack does not cause physical pain in most cases.

You quickly modify your behavior in the physical domain if you feel threatened. A prowler going around the block will cause you to lock your windows, even when the breeze outside is fantastic.

Law enforcement officers and responders seem to be creatures of habit when it comes to eating in the same restaurant. While you are enjoying your meals, with your Bluetooth **On** and Location Services also **On**, any knucklehead or a member of a drug cartel, can pwn you.

Let's return our attention to Figure 9 - Apple Settings Screen, and click on **Cellular**. I want to bring your attention to the **Personal Hotspot** option. The Personal Hotspot acts as a Wi-Fi connection. It is a secure connection, and my first choice to use on my computer when I am out and about, instead of using someone else's Wi-Fi connection, such as that of the establishment I'm visiting.

How does the Personal Hotspot work? It is a more secure way to connect your tablet or computer (regardless the operating system: Apple or Windows, etc.) to the Internet when you are not at home. Instead of using an unsecure connection such as a hotel or restaurant's Wi-Fi, you can use a Personal Hotspot. To connect, click on the **Personal Hotspot** option on your device. A page shows up with the following options:

> **Allow Others to Join – ** Turn this ON
>
> **Wi-Fi Password**: xxxxx ➔ Whatever collection of letters and numbers your phone is showing here is the password that you will need to enter on the Wi-Fi of your computer to connect.

Now, on your computer, go to the Wi-Fi icon to select a network. Your iPhone should be listed there. Select it, and enter the Wi-Fi password that your phone shows (see above).

Note that you can also connect to a Personal Hotspot using a USB cable. Of course, you will have the option to use Bluetooth for the connection. But because you are now cyber-educated about the dangers of Bluetooth, you will bypass that option.

Let's continue hardening your Apple device. On the upper left corner of your device, click on the blue title, **Cellular**. Now, we are again on the **Cellular** page. Make sure you select **On** for the option **Wi-Fi Calling**. When you are connected to Wi-Fi, you will not use cellular data but the free Wi-Fi connection. It is up to you whether you want or do not want to receive calls on other devices.

Now, scroll down the page, and you will see all the apps running on your phone. If you have unlimited cellular data usage, you can have all the apps in green. However, if you have limited data usage, you must look at each of these apps and decide which is essential for you to consume cellular data when you are away from your home or office and do not have a Wi-Fi connection.

Scroll to the very end of that long list of apps, and ensure the option **Wi-Fi Assist** is **ON.**

On the upper left corner of your screen, touch the blue title, **Settings**, to go back one page.

On the **Settings** page, you will see the **VPN** option. We will learn more about VPNs later in the book. (See CHAPTER 6 - VIRTUAL PRIVATE NETWORKS.)

The next change we need to make has to do with the notifications of your text messages. Select the **Notifications** title.

On the **Notifications** page, click on the option, **Show Previews,** and select, **When Unlocked**. This means that when your phone is locked, you will receive an audible notification whenever a message has arrived from any of your apps. However, you will need to enter your phone password to unlock your phone and read that message. I will explain why shortly. Stay with me on this page, because we need to make one more change. Scroll down the list of apps until you find **Messages**. Click on it, and the **Messages** page shows on the screen.

On the **Message** page, select **Immediate Delivery**. Turn ON the options, **Critical Alerts** and **Time Sensitive Notifications**. Then, scroll down to the end of that page, and under the title **Show Previews**, select again the option **When Unlocked**.

Social engineering (see Social Engineering) is one of the techniques hackers use to steal your information. Imagine that you are in a public place. Your phone is face-up on a table or the bar, and as messages come into your phone and displays a preview on the screen, even when the phone is locked, anyone near you can start reading the name of the sender and parts of the message. Now, imagine you also have your Bluetooth on, and this unscrupulous person trying to take advantage of your lack of cyber security. The hacker decides to Bluesnarf you (see definition above). A few minutes later, a text comes in from one of your friends begging you to send money right away because this friend of yours is in a life-threatening situation. This is the hacker trying to steal your money.

Hopefully, now you better understand why it is so important to shut off Bluetooth, and also keep incoming messages privately while the phone is locked.

Now, touch the blue title, **Notifications,** in the upper left corner. Select **Settings** to return to the original **Settings** page.

Look for the title, **General,** and click on it. This takes you to the **General** page, where you can see information about your phone when you click the **About** option. Click on **Software Update.** The device gives you a few options when you click on it. Apple has released some updates with serious flaws in the past. Therefore, I prefer to automatically install only the Security Responses & Systems Files but not the iOS Updates.

On the second window below those options, you will see the option, "Automatically Download." I have selected green for iOS Updates. In other words, when the iOS Updates feature is green, that means Apple will tell me when there is an upgrade available. I do a quick look online to find out whether that upgrade has problems. If nothing pops up, I install the upgrade.

Let's go back to the **General** page. Select the title, **AirPlay & Handoff.** On the page that pops up, the option that presents a security problem is **Handoff.** Turn this option OFF. This is another way to compartmentalized your devices, which I addressed earlier in the book. You do not want to carry your activities from one device to another automatically. Should your iPhone get infected with malware, you do not want to also infect your computer, iPad, etc.

On the upper left corner of the screen, touch the blue title, **General**. On this page, at the very bottom, you see the title, **Transfer or Reset iPhone**. Click on that and at the bottom of the page, you will see two more options: **Reset** and **Erase All Content and Settings.** Should you suspect that your device has been seriously compromised., this option allows you to return your phone to factory settings and erase its contents completely.

For example, a person who has a problem with you (an ex, for example) might send you a photo that you have to download in order to view. Once you download it, you cannot delete from your device. This could mean that the photo had malware, and now the person who sent it to you has full control of your phone.

To regain secure control of your device, touch the **Erase All Content and Settings.** Be aware that, by selecting this option, you will lose all the data that was not included in your last backup. (This is a good time to again remind you of the importance of backing up your devices frequently.)

Now, touch the blue title, **General,** and then select the blue title, **Settings**.

Scroll down until you find the title, **Face ID & Passcode**. Click on it, and enter the passcode to unlock the phone. If you have enabled the feature **FACE ID FOR** any of the options listed under that title, turn them off. The most secure way to unlock your devices is a passcode, not any of your physical features (eyes, finger, face).

Why shouldn't you use biometrics (face, fingers, etc.) to unlock devices? Because anyone can knock you unconscious, put the phone to your face or your finger and open it. In fact, you don't even need to be unconscious for a malicious person to force you to unlock your phone.

Continue scrolling down on this page, and select **Require Passcode Immediately**. Under the **ALLOW ACCESS WHEN LOCKED** title, ensure all of those options are grayed out.

Let's go back to the main **Settings** page, and select the title **Privacy & Security** option. By now, you should have **Location Services** turn On. Leave Location Services ON for now while we make some other changes on this page. Select the option, **Tracking,** and gray it out. Then, select the options, **Photos, Microphone,** and **Camera.** Open each of these to see which apps you have given access to your photos, microphone, and camera. Ask yourself if all these apps really need to have access to your photos, your microphone AND your camera. Most likely, you will be able to deny access to many.

Keep scrolling down on that page, and you will see, almost at the end, the option, **Analytics & Improvements**. Click on that option and turn off all the options provided. Then, on that same screen, click on the option, **Analytics Data**. You will see the operating system of your phone. As a car aficionado would say, you are now looking "under the hood." This is very important because if you suspect that your phone has been hacked, a cyber security expert will ask you to look at these processes and might ask you to send screen shots of them.

Now, in the upper left corner, and as you have done before many times, click back twice to land again on the **Security & Privacy** page. Click on **Location Services,** and be sure it is turned ON. When you turn this feature ON, a long list of apps appears on the bottom of the page.

On all the apps; with the exception of navigation apps and banking apps such as Square, select the option, **Never**. There is no need for you to disclose your location to a bunch of apps that have no need to know. On your navigation and banking apps, select the navigation option **While Using**.

On this same page, scroll further down until you see, **System Services**, and click on it. Follow the settings you see options similar to Figure 12 – System Services.

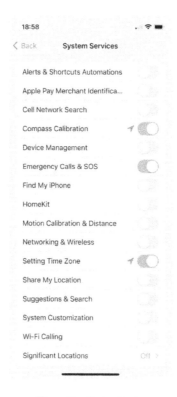

Figure 12 – System Services

Look for the option, "Significant Locations" and select it. If your Significant Locations is ON, select the **Clear History** option. Then, turn Significant Locations **Off**. See Figure 13 - Significant Locations

Figure 13 - Significant Locations

Now, continue to scroll down the **System Services** page until you see, **iPhone Analytics.** Turn **iPhone Analytics** OFF. Also turn OFF the **Improve Maps** function. Leave ON the **Routing & Traffic** and **Status Bar Icon.**

In the upper left corner, click the blue title, **Back,** to return to the **Location Services** screen, and turn **Location Services OFF.** Unless you are using a navigation app, there is no need for you to have Location Services on and broadcasting your whereabouts all over the map. When you need a navigation app such as Waze or Maps to help you reach a destination, then go to the Location Services screen, turn Location Services ON. Then, turn Location Services OFF once you reach your destination. This is another situation where you might want to put a yellow sticky note on your dashboard to remind you to turn Location Services OFF.

Congratulations! Having followed these instructions, your Apple devices are now hardened. Now, let's back up those devices.

Backing up your Apple devices to an Apple Computer

Backing up your system is important because if you lose your data, you always have a backup copy to recover that data. You can lose the data if you phone/tablet or computer is stolen. The backup is also very useful when your phone or computer is hacked. The hacker sends you a ransomware demand for you to pay, and for the hacker to give you access again to your data. However, if you have that data backed up, you do not need to pay because you have your own data backed up.

On your Mac computer, select the **Finder** app (see image below)

When the **Finder** window opens and your phone is plugged in to the computer, find **Locations** in the left column. There, you will find your phone and/or tablet listed. (Note that you can do this with the tablet, as well. See Figure 14.

Figure 14 – Finder Screen

Click on the device you want to back up. Figure 14 shows what you will see. On the right column, top, you will see titles such as, "General," "Music," etc. Click on **General**. You can then click on **Check for Updates** if you have not updated your device operating system lately. (As a reminder, you should regularly update your operating system.)

Under the **Backups** section, select **Back up all of the data** and **Encrypt local backup**. You will be asked to create a password. This password should be 16 character long. Write it on a piece of paper and secure that paper inside a physical safe box. (See CHAPTER 1 - PASSWORDS if you need a reminder on how to create a secure password.)

Then, select **Back Up Now**.

Under **Options**, you can select options as you please. Notice in Figure 14 I have selected the manual management of my music, movies, and TV shows.

At the very bottom of the screen, you will see the progress bar once the backup begins.

How often should you back up your phone/tablet? At the minimum, you should back it up monthly. However, anytime you add a lot of information to your device (such as if you attend a meeting or take a trip), then you should back up your phone.

Why are these backups so important? Because they will protect your data from any hacker with a ransom malware where the hacker locks your phone and asks for money to give you back the access to your data. In other words, you won't lose any data on your device when that data is backed up, because it is stored in an encrypted backup. So, worst case scenario if you get hacked would be that you need a new phone, to which you will bring your encrypted backed-up data. Assuming you perform regular backups on your device, you will lose at the most the few pieces of data you added to your device from the time of the last backup to the moment you were served a ransomware attack.

DO NOT pay the ransom. Why? Because by paying, you continue to enable these types of attacks. because And these attacks they are very, very lucrative. Data is not like a bicycle. When a thief steals your bike or any other physical possession, you report the crime to the police and hopefully they help you recover the item. When data is stolen, it is in the hands of bad actors forever. Even if you pay the ransom, and you get receive access to your phone again, all of your data remains is in the hands of the hacker, who will continue using it to exploit you and more people.

Backing up your Apple devices to a Windows computer

If you have never backed up your Apple device to a Windows computer, you will first need to download the iTunes app to your Windows computer. To do so, follow these steps:

1. Close all open apps on your Windows computer

2. Open a browser and go to the iTunes Download page (https://support.apple.com/en-us/118290)

3. Click "Get it from Microsoft"

4. Click "Get"

5. Click "Save"

6. Select the location where you would like to store the file and click "Save" again

7. Once the download is complete, click "Run"

8. If prompted, click "Next" and select an option

9. Click "Install"

10. If prompted to allow changes, click "Yes"

11. Click "Finish"

Once the iTunes app is installed on your Windows computer, do the following:

1. Connect your Apple device (iPhone/iPad, etc) to your Windows computer using the cable that came with your Apple device. Note that you might have to visit the Apple store to get a cable that has two different types of connections, if your cable does not fit the Windows computer.

2. Open the iTunes app on your Windows computer.

3. Click the button for the Apple device you see near the top left of the iTunes window.

4. Click **Summary**.

5. Click Back Up Now (below **Backups**).

6. Select **Encrypt local backup.** Type a password using the technique described in the previous chapter, then click **Set Password**. Again,

this password should be 16 characters long. Write it on a piece of paper and secure that paper inside a physical safe box.

Note that Backups made using iTunes will include your text messages, notes, the phone call history, contact favorites, sound settings, widget settings, and the photos stored in Camera Roll or Saved Photos. Songs, videos, and some photos do not get backed up, but can be restored by syncing with iTunes; thus, you will not lose anything.

How often should you back up your phone/tablet? At the minimum, monthly; however, if you attend a meeting and add much information or take a trip and have a bunch of new data, then back up your phone more often as your lifestyle dictates.

Why are these backups so important? Because if you ever get hacked with a ransom malware where the hacker locks your phone and asks for money to give you the access to your data back, you can flip the hacker because you have all of your data in an encrypted backup. So, worst case scenario is that you need a new phone where you will bring your encrypted backed up data. At the most, you will lose the few things you added to your device from the time of the last backup to the moment you were served a ransomware attack.

DO NOT pay the ransom. Why? Because by paying, you continue to enable these types of attacks because they are very, very lucrative. Data is not like a bicycle. When a thief steals your bike or any other physical possession, you report the crime to the police and hopefully they help you recover the item. When data is stolen, it is in the hands of bad actors forever. Even if you pay the ransom, and you get access to your phone again, all of your data is in the hands of a hacker who will continue use it to exploit you and more people.

Android Smartphones and Tablets

Android devices are considered more vulnerable to hackers because these devices use an open-source code operating system (meaning anyone can modify the code in spite of efforts to police the open-source community), and cost less than Apple devices. Therefore, they are more ubiquitous. If a hacker creates malware, the hacker will likely release it to an environment where there will be more return on investment. Given that there are more Android devices in the world than Apple devices, many malicious attacks are designed for the Android operating system.

Next time you need to replace your phone and/or tablet, I recommend that you buy Apple devices.[15]

From the Google Play store, download, install and run the application Malwarebytes. This is an excellent anti-virus that will assist you in protecting the cyber perimeter of your phone. Once you know that your phone is free of viruses, proceed to the steps below to harden it.

Once we are done securing your Android phone and tablet, we will encrypt both. Thus, if your Android device is stolen or you leave it in a public place, anyone who gets it will not be able to steal its contents because the device is encrypted. It is as if someone takes your purse and the contents inside are completely worthless to the thief.

Because the Android operating system is embedded in so many different brands, each brand has its own user interface. A Samsung phone looks different than a Google phone, for example, but both use the same operating system. Therefore, it is not practical in this section to illustrate the explanations with images of user interfaces, because there are so many. Instead, I will share with you what features to look for in your own device and how to adjust them. I am always open to scheduling one-on-one or group classes if you'd like more thorough help. You can schedule a one-on-one or group class via my website at www.anastosresearch.com.

Regardless of the user interface of your phone, we will look first at your **Network & Internet** option. Note that you can enable your Hotspot to connect securely to your computer instead of using a Wi-Fi that you do not own (see page 29 for more on Hotspots) . Make sure that your network connection is set to WPA2 and has a 16-character password.

Once you create your account for the virtual private network (VPN) (CHAPTER 6 - VIRTUAL PRIVATE NETWORKS), remember to come

---

[15] I am not being financially compensated to promote Apple products. I recommend them because I believe they are better than the competition.

back to Settings on your mobile devices to enable the VPN.

Now, let's take a look at the **Connected devices**. You want to monitor this periodically to ensure that nobody is piggybacking on your technology.

Back in the **Settings** screen, touch **Notifications**. I recommend that you receive previews of notifications (text message notifications in particular) ONLY when your device is unlocked. This means that when your phone is locked, you will hear the sound that a message has arrived from any of your apps that have notification sounds enabled; however, you will need to enter your phone password to unlock the phone and read that message.

Social engineering (see Social Engineering) is one of the techniques hackers use to steal your information. Imagine that you are in a public place, your phone is face up on a table or the bar, and as messages come into your phone and show a preview on the screen, even when the phone is locked, anyone near you can start reading the name of the sender and parts of the message. Then, imagine you also have your Bluetooth on, and this unscrupulous person trying to take advantage of your lack of cyber security, decides to Bluesnarf you (see definition above). A few minutes later, a text comes in from one of your friends begin you to send money right away because this friend of yours is in a pickle, bla,bla… it is the hacker trying to steal your money.

Hopefully, now you understand better why it is so important to shut that Bluetooth, and also to keep incoming messages privately while the phone is locked.

Talking about **Bluetooth**, look for that setting on your device and turn it **OFF**.[16] Bluetooth is the weakest link of any device; in particular, when you are in a public place like gym, airports, restaurants, etc. This is because the OBEX protocol in the Bluetooth, when it is open to communicate with another device, such as your headphone or car speaker, does not have nor does it require authentication policies.

Therefore, a knucklehead sitting within 10 feet of you, and pretending to be busy with a computer or even a little device called Raspberry, can hack your

---

[16] If you wear a lifesaving wearable such as a glucose monitor, you will not be able to turn your Bluetooth off. Be extra aware of text sent to you from numbers you do not recognize, and do not click on any link or photos sent to you via those text messages from unknown parties.

open Bluetooth connection.

There are several types of Bluetooth hacking:

- Bluebagging: Unauthorized control of your device
- Bluesnarfing: A hacker, using your open Bluetooth connection, steals your emails contacts, text messages, photos.
- Bluejacking: You will receive unsolicited message from a hacker near you. It is more annoying than dangerous, unless the messages contain a link infected with malware.
- Man-in-the-Middle (or the not so fun ménage-à-trois of technology): A hacker intercepts all of your communications, and this person can also manipulate them by redirecting you to a look-alike page of a bank, for example.

Earlier on the book, I talked about behavior modification. The use of Bluetooth and Location Services are the best examples of your willingness to make a conscious effort to modify behavior. If you want to use the Bluetooth while you are driving, the risk is slightly less because it would be hard to catch you while in movement. The question is, will you have the mindfulness, in other words, the presence of your mind in the moment of parking the vehicle and think about security measures to protect your cyber perimeter? You might have to begin by placing yellow stickies on the dashboard of your vehicle that read "Turn BT OFF," and "Turn Location Service OFF," once you reach your destination.

Is this a pain in the rear end? Yes, for some who are used to Bluetoothing their lives off, it could be. Is it different than having to use other protective measures in the physical domain to safeguard you? No. I would love to get out of my car and not having to lock it. We live in a world where that is no longer possible unless you leave in the middle of bloody nowhere.

Why is it so difficult to change cyber behavior? Because the hack does not cause physical pain in most cases; unless, you are connected to tubes in a hospital that got hacked and the machine stopped working.

You quickly modify your behavior in the physical domain if you feel threatened. A prowler going around the block will make you lock your windows even when the breeze outside is fantastic.

Law enforcement officers and responders seem to be creatures of habit when it comes to eating in the same restaurant. While you are enjoying your meals, with your Bluetooth **On** and Location Services also **On**, any knucklehead or a member of a drug cartel, can pwn you.

Now, let's look at **Security & Privacy**. If you have been using your face or fingerprint to unlock your device, I highly recommend that you cancel that and replace with a pattern or passcode.

Why shouldn't you use biometrics (face, fingers, etc.) to unlock devices? Because anyone can knock you unconscious, put the phone to your face or your finger and open it. In fact, you don't even need to be unconscious for a malicious person to force you to unlock your phone.

On the **App Security** ensure to turn on the Play Protect scanning.

Now, look for **Device finders** and ensure to turn this off. Yes, you have read it correctly. This option is one of the biggest holes in security for electronic devices. If you can find your phone, so the hackers.

If you are concerned about misplacing the phone within your house or office, I suggest you buy this amazing clip made by Aduro. The clip allows you to attack it to your clothing regardless whether you wear a dress or pants. When I wear dresses, I attached the clip to the necklace of the dress.

Aduro Combo Case & Holster.

You also need to look at the **Permission Manager**. Note that your device might use a different name for this feature, it is the permissions you grant to apps, and to whom you allow to use your camera, photos and microphone.

From the main **Settings** screen, let's look at **Location.** You want to have your location services always off; except, when you are using a navigator.

Finally, we are ready to encrypt your Android device. If you do not know where this feature is in the Settings screen, type it in the search bar of your **Settings** screen, and you will soon discover its location. Encrypt the device.

This is all I have to write about the Android.

Apple Computers

The operating system of the Apple computer used to be completely different than those of the iPhone and iPad. With the release of the Sonoma operating system, Apple practically replicated the iPhone/iPad operating system user interface into its computers. Therefore, the principles discussed in the previous section about many of the security features also apply to the Apple computers.

Before we begin hardening your computer, it is important that you install the anti-virus Malwarebytes. It is not on the Apple store (at the time of writing this book). You need to go to the website https://www.malwarebytes.com/mac-download and download it from there.

Once you download the software and install it in your Mac, you will see a letter M on the upper right corner of your computer. Click it and run the anti-virus to ensure your computer is clean. Once you have secured and analyzed the computer, continue reading to begin hardening your device.

On your Apple computer, open the **Systems Preferences** page, which you can access by clicking on the gray symbol where your apps show, or by clicking on the Apple symbol located on the upper left corner of your screen, and selecting **System Preferences**. See Figure 15 - System Preferences.

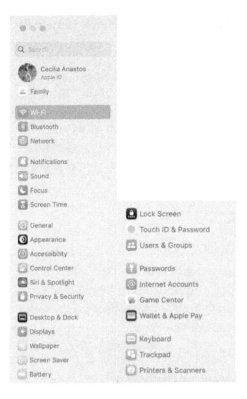

Figure 15 - System Preferences

On the upper left corner of the **System Preferences** screen, click on **Apple ID.** A new page pops up on the right panel. Visit each one of those options and adjust accordingly to what it was discussed in the previous section for Apple devices (see Apple Smartphones and Tablets).

Close the Wi-Fi window.

Now, on the left panel, touch **Wi-Fi.** On the screen to the right, you see your Wi-Fi connection and the option, **Details,** to the far right. Enable the option, **Limit IP address tracking**. On that same screen, at the bottom left, you will see the title, **Forget this Network**. When does this feature come handy? Let's say that you decide to work at a coffee shop and you connect to their network. Once you are done with your work, you want your computer to forget the network you were working on. This way, when you pass that coffee shop with your laptop again, the laptop will not automatically connect to that Wi-Fi. You should always select the **Forget this Network** option after you use a public Wi-Fi network. You always want to be in control of which Wi-Fi you are connecting to. Now, close the Wi-Fi window.

On the left panel, select **Bluetooth** and turn it **Off.** Whenever Apple upgrades your computer, it turns the Bluetooth on without your consent. Thus, this is something you need to monitor each time you install an upgrade. For more on why Bluetooth should be turned off, see my explanation on page 28.

Next, on the left panel, click on **Network.** On the right panel, you will see **Wi-Fi**. Click on that title, **Wi-Fi**, scroll to the bottom of the panel, and disable **Ask to join networks.** This is because you do not want your computer to join networks automatically. You want to always be in control of that selection. On top of the screen, touch the left arrow < to return to the **Network** page. Select **Firewall** and make sure you have enabled it. If the firewall is enabled, you should see the button in blue. To the right, you will see the title, **Options.** Click on it and a new window pops up. At the bottom of that window, you see **Enable stealth mode**. Make sure this mode is turned on (blue). Click **Cancel** to exit that screen and touch the arrow on the upper left corner to go back one more screen.

On the left panel, select **Notifications** and apply the concepts you learned in the previous section (Apple Smartphones and Tablets)

On the left, select **General**. Almost at the end of the right panel, you will see the title **Time Machine**. This is what you will use to back up your computer, and we will discuss this in detail later in the book. (See Backing up your Apple computer.)

On the left panel, touch **Privacy & Security.** We discussed privacy and security extensively in the previous section (see Apple Smartphones and Tablets). On the computer, it has a few features different from the Smartphone and Tablet. When you scroll down the right panel, for example, you'll see the **Security** title. Below it, select **App Store and identified developers** to download important software outside the Apple store, such as Malwarebytes.

Look for **FileVault** and click on it to turn it on. This feature encrypts your entire computer. Thus, if your laptop or desktop is stolen, or you leave it behind in a public place, whoever gets it will not be able to steal its contents. Just like with a Smartphone or Tablet, if someone steals your computer and your computer is encrypted, it is as if someone takes your purse and the contents inside are entirely foreign and therefore worthless to the thief.

When you click on **Turn On** to enable the FileVault, Apple will show you a screen with a long secret key. Apple offers you to place that into the keychain. Say **No**. You want to take a photo of that, print it on paper, and put it on your safe. Putting this secret key in the keychain is like having a little paper inside your purse explaining what each object is. You want to keep that secret key in a safe place, and separately from the computer.

Now, let's return our attention to the left panel. Select **Touch ID & Password**. If you have added your fingerprint here, remove that option and select **Password** only. Make sure you follow the principles you learned in CHAPTER 1 - PASSWORDS.

On the left panel, select **Passwords**. Enter your computer password to unlock this feature, and, if you have allowed the computer to save any passwords, this is where you will see them. Ensure you turn off the iCloud Keychain. If you have reused passwords, the **Security Recommendations** feature lists all the websites where you have used the same password. I recommend changing recycled passwords as soon as possible.

On the **Password Options**, at the bottom of the page, ensure you have enabled the **Delete After Use**. This will delete the verification codes in Messages and Mail after they are used. If you have difficulty remembering passwords, you can enable the **AutoFill Passwords and Passkeys**. However, do not use this with your financial, email accounts, or health records. You want to have exclusive control of the access to those services; therefore, you should always enter those passwords manually.

For my default web browser, I prefer to use DuckDuckGo. You will learn more about the different web browsers in CHAPTER 9 – SURFING THE WEB UNDETECTED.

Backing up your Apple computer

To back up your computer, you will need an external hard drive. My favorite is *WD 2TB My Passport for Mac, Portable External Hard Drive with backup software and password protection, USB 3.1/USB 3.0 compatible.* The 2TB means that the capacity of this hard drive is two terabytes. If you collect a lot of movies, you might want to purchase a higher capacity such as 3TB.

Once you have the external hard drive, turn on your computer. On the upper left corner of the screen, touch the Apple symbol and select **Systems**

Settings. Go to **General** and select **Time Machine**. A new screen displays on the right-hand panel, asking you to **Add Backup Disk**. Connect your external hard drive to your computer. A small window pops up showing the name of your external hard drive and an option on the bottom right, **Set Up Disk**. Click **Set Up Disk** and, on the screen that pops up, enable the **Encrypt Backup** by turning the button to blue. Create a password following the guidelines in CHAPTER 1 - PASSWORDS. (Don't forget to write a hint for the password.) Click **Done**. Once the backup is completed, disconnect the external drive from your computer and put it inside a safe box.

The backup you have just created contains the contents of your computer, as well as the contents of your iPhone/iPad because you also backed up this data to your computer. Now, if anything happens to your phone or computer, you can restore that data from the backup.

Make a note on your calendar to back up your technology at least one a month.

PC Computers

For the PC computers, I will only address the Windows environment because it is the operating system that most people use. Nevertheless, the principles of privacy I describe for the Windows environment will also apply to other operating systems.

Before we harden your device, you need to install an anti-virus software if you have not done so already. My favorite is Malwarebytes.com

Once you have installed and run the anti-virus, click on the Windows logo in the lower left corner of your computer and then click on **Settings**. Select **System, Notifications & Actions**. Ensure you remove the check mark from **Show notifications on the lock screen**. You do not want anyone to be able to read notifications from your computer when the screen is locked.

Return to the **Settings** page, and select **Bluetooth & Devices**. Make sure your Bluetooth is **OFF** when you are taking this computer outside of your home.

From the **Settings** page, select **Network & Internet**. Turn the **Firewall ON**. Then, click on **Wi-Fi** and turn **On** the features, **Use random hardware addresses** and the **Hotspot**.

Back on the **Settings** page, select **Privacy.** On the right-hand panel, select **General.** Turn off, **Let apps use advertising….**, and the other three features below that. On the left panel, select **Activity History**, and remove the check mark from both options. You will also want to turn off the activity history for your account and clear the activity history at the bottom of the page.

On the left panel, select **Location** and ensure it is **OFF** for all the options listed on that page. You also need to clear the location history on the device.

Backing up your PC computer

You will need an external hard drive where you will back up your computer. My favorite is *WD 2TB My Passport for Mac, Portable External Hard Drive with backup software and password protection, USB 3.1 / USB 3.0 compatible.* The 2TB means that the capacity of this hard drive is two terabytes. If you collect a lot of movies, you might want to purchase a higher capacity such as 3TB.

Once you have the external hard drive in your hands, open your computer, plug the external hard drive on the computer, and follow these steps:

- From the lower left corner, touch the Windows log, select **Settings**, and go to "**System**" → "**Storage**" → "**Advanced storage settings**" → "**Backup options**"

- Select "**Add a drive**" (under "**Backup using File History**")

- Toggle the "**On**" switch under "**Automatically back up my files**"

- Choose "**More options**" to configure File History specifics, which includes options for how frequently you want to back up your PC.

Once you have backed up your PC, disconnect the hard drive and place it somewhere safe.

I do not trust the OneDrive to back up anything. I recommend using Dropbox. See CHAPTER 5 – ENCRYPTED STORAGE.

Configuring your Wi-Fi Router

Configuring your Wi-Fi router is one of the most important aspects of your cyber perimeter.

When you sign up with an internet service provider such as Cox Communications, Spectrum , etc., the service provider usually gives you the option to use one of their modems and routers for a monthly fee. Those have been used over and over again by other customers, and who knows the dirt that has passed through them. In fact, in the book, *Cyber War,* (https://amzn.to/3yPEtEE), authors Richard Clarke and Robert Knake claim that AT&T knows the equipment they provide is infected with malware, but the company does not tell you for fear of losing you as a customer. Because of this, I recommend that you always purchase your own modem and routerGuess what? AT&T does not allow you to do that. I strongly suggest that you sign up with a provider that allows you to use your own modem and router.

You will need to know how to access your router because you will need to configure different passwords for each of your Wi-Fi channels. It's also important that you regularly update your router's operating system. There are many brands of routers on the market, and each has its own way of letting you see what it is inside the router. For some, like Netgear, you must open a browser and type, "routerlogin.net" in the URL bar. . For other brands, you will be asked to enter the router's IP address, which is always printed somewhere on the device.

All routers come with a default factory password, or a password written outside the box. DO NOT use the default password. The first thing you should do when you buy a router is to change the master password. The username will, by default, be **admin** (usually all lowercase), and the default password, believe it or not, is often the word **password** (usually in lowercase). Even if your router comes with a preset username and password that is more sophisticated than this, you will need to change the password to a 16-character password, applying the techniques in CHAPTER 1 - PASSWORDS.

Once you log into the router with your newly created secure username and password, you will see something similar to **Error! Reference source not found.**.

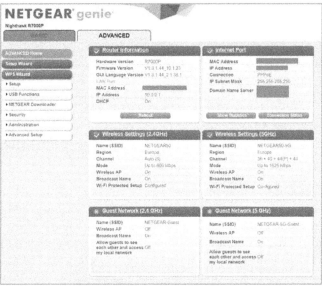

Figure 16 - Netgear Router User Interface

For the sake of example, and because images help when trying to understand technology, let's assume that you have a Netgear router.

All routers these days give you four channels: Wireless 2.4 GHz; Wireless 5GHz; Guest network 2.4 GHz; and Guest Network 5 GHz. For each of these channels, you will need to change the Name (SSID) so nobody from outside the house can see what brand of router you have. Do not use your own name, or your pet's name. Come up with something that you have not posted in social media, etc. Some people with wit were changing the SSIDs with names such as FBI Surveillance, NSA, etc. Use your imagination here.

Also, for each of these channels, you will create a different password. The passwords of your Wi-Fi router are critical to be kept secure. Therefore, these are not passwords that you should allow any password manager to remember. Write a hint for each password and keep that hint somewhere safe, but never write the password itself down.

Now, you have four different Wi-Fi channels, and you will allocate them as follows:

1. If you have children at home, give them the Wireless 5GHz which tends to be faster. This way, the kids will not try to steal the password of the faster network and create a mess.

2. For the Internet of Things such as Alexa, and for anyone visiting the home and wanting to connect to your Wi-Fi. It is also a good idea to use this network for Alexa or another wireless home system. For you and your spouse/partner, use the Wireless 5GHz.
3. For you and your spouse/partner, use the Wireless 5GHz
4. For your security cameras, use the Wireless 2.4GHz.

As you click on all the titles you see on the user interface of your router, ensure you select WPA2 as your type of security. Do not allow guests to see each other on the network. Log in to this device regularly to ensure that only your devices are connected to any of the Wi-Fi channels, and to update the operating system whenever the manufacturer issues an update/upgrade.

The access to your Wi-Fi router is similar to the keylocks of your home. Only allow access to people you trust completely. If you give someone a key to your house and then trust is later lost or your relationship with that person sours, you will likely change the locks on your doors. You should do the same with your Wi-Fi router, and immediately. I have helped many women whose lives were turned upside down because an ex-partner was hacking them through the Wi-Fi box.

In fact, it will not hurt if you also check your home for potential hidden cameras. The model X13 is equipped with even GPS tracker so you can check whether one is placed underneath your vehicle. I recommend this one, available on Amazon, or one with a similar functionality: https://amzn.to/4cJ9sQG. Use it to sweep your home, hotel rooms and rental homes.

Figure 17 - Camera / GPS Detector https://amzn.to/4cJ9sQG

CHAPTER 4 – ENCRYPTED COMMUNICATIONS

Encrypted communications are a must to avoid having the man-in-the-middle problem; i.e., someone learning details about your life which can be used to exploit you financially through social engineering scams and/or blackmail; someone learning details about a crime scene, person of interest, etc. that could jeopardize the successful prosecution of the case.

If you own an Apple device and you text another Apple device, your message is, by default, equipped with end-to-end encryption. This means that no one can read your messages as they travel between the two Apple devices. If law enforcement serves a search warrant to Apple, Inc., requesting to read your messages, Apple, Inc., will have nothing to show because these messages are encrypted. Apple, Inc., does not have a copy of your messages anywhere. The only way to read these messages is to have access to *your* device. The only thing Apple, Inc., will be able to provide is a history of phones your Apple device has texted/called. It will have none of the content.

If you own an Apple device and you text an Android device, the encryption feature is gone. Text messages between Apple devices are blue. Text messages between Apple and Android devices are green. If you live close to the border with Mexico or Canada, your phone, even though it is an Apple phone, could be picking up a foreign tower. If you send text messages from an Apple phone to another Apple phone near either of these borders and one or both of the phones is utilizing a foreign tower, the text messages will be green – which, again, means no encryption.

When I teach my cyber defense classes, I often hear comments such as, "I am only texting my child (or grandchild)," or, "nobody is interested in what I have to say."

Actually, many bad actors are trying to exploit the seemingly trivial things you share through your phone. According to the FBI, in 2023, cybercrime in the United States jumped 22%, giving hackers $12.5 billion in earnings.

If each of us maintains a proper cyber defense aided by technology and behavior, hackers would not be raking in this amount of money from American citizens. It is important that you be part of the solution and adopt technologies and behaviors that will cause hackers to move on and leave you alone.

I know that some of the changes I recommend here are inconvenient. But, if you think about these changes in terms of being a patriot and taking action for the greater good – not doing simply what is convenient for you – then you will reap the value from these sometimes monotonous, sometimes inconvenient tasks. When you harden your cyber perimeter, everybody wins, except hackers.

Encrypted Apps for Texting and Calls

If you have WhatsApp on your phone, remove it right away. It is the worst app you can have on your phone for security reasons. Even though you might read that it has end-to-end encryption, don't trust it. Whatever you write in WhatsApp goes through the Meta servers, where anything you write can be exploited for commercial purposes, such as sending you marketing for products that Meta's Artificial Intelligence servers might think you need. Take a look at https://faq.whatsapp.com/1303762270462331https://faq.whatsapp.com/1303762270462331 where the company explains all the things it collects from you. When you use WhatsApp, your privacy is the product.

Moreover, when law enforcement serves a search warrant to Meta to look at a WhatsApp account, Meta gives them a copy of everything that the person in trouble with the law has written there. How about if you are dating a criminal and you do not know anything about his/her criminal activities? All of your texts end up in the open because law enforcement requested a search warrant to look at everything that person had texted in WhatsApp. Oops… there goes your privacy as well (photos included).

We know there isn't good coordination/cooperation between different law enforcement departments/agencies. Imagine this situation where you are working on undercover capacity, and you are using WhatsApp from everywhere, and you take that phone with you to your home, and it will pick up your home Wi-Fi and IP address. Then, unbeknown to you, a different agency presents a search warrant to a member of the criminal organization you are watching, all the WhatsApp data ends up in the open including your text, home IP address, etc.

If you are using Telegram, also get out of there. It is a cesspool. It will put you in the same dangerous situation I described above. As I am writing this book, Telegram's CEO has been arrested by French authorities for his negligence in allowing illicit activity in Telegram.

If you need to use these apps (WhatsApp and Telegram) as part of your work, then have the department issue you a work phone that you will only use for work related activities. Before you go home, you put it on a Faraday bag, and it stays there until you leave your home and you start your shift again.

Best app for texting encrypted is Signal (https://signal.org/) which you can download from the Apple Store and Google Play (you will learn how to set it up in a few paragraphs below, How to Configure Signal). This is a free app, no charge to use the services it provides. This is the best app for everyday texting, regardless of your profession. It also allows you to create groups, make phone calls using Wi-Fi or cellular data, best app to communicate with your family and friends when you are traveling abroad.

If you are looking for the best app for encrypted calls and text, including file sharing, for your department, I recommend Silent Circle (https://www.silentcircle.com/)

How to Configure Signal

Go to the Apple Store or Google Play, select **Signal – Private Messenger** and download on your device. It will ask you to create an account using your cellphone number. Once you have created your account, touch the icon on the upper left corner, and select **Settings.** On top, you will see your name and phone number. Click on that, and select a photo or an icon to use to identify yourself (or you can leave it blank and Signal will use the first letter of your name), and a Username if you do not want people to see your phone number.

On the upper left corner, click the < to go back one screen. You can install it also on your iPad and computer and you will see all devices linked to your account when you click on **Linked Devices**.

Click on **Chats** and gray out all of those options. Notice the red title at the bottom, **Clear Chat History**. At any given moment, you can touch this bottom and all of your conversations that you see on the screen go away forever.

Next, let's look at the **Privacy** option. A new screen comes up, select **Phone Number**, and mark **Nobody** on the **Who can see my number**. For the option **Who can find me by number**, I leave it up to your choice. Keep in mind that if anyone text you here from a number that you do not know, ignore it. This app is secure to the max and the only thing that can break that security is your behavior, such as accepting texts from phone numbers you do not know, and clicking on links sent via those texts.

Let's go back one screen to be in the **Privacy** screen again. Notice the **Blocked** title. There you will see the list of phone numbers/people you have blocked.

I prefer to have the **Read Receipts** on the **Off** position so nobody knows whether I have or haven't read the texts, and removes the pressure of having to reply immediately. I have also turned off the **Typing Indicators**.

For **Disappearing Messages,** you can set a general time for all the messages equally. For example, if you turn it on, you can say that all the messages, regardless who is texting with you, stay live on the app for 15 minutes or 1 hour, and then they all disappear. You can also set this feature individually for every person who chats with you here. You might want to keep the messages from family and clients forever, but those from your dates to disappear at an amount of time that you want.

To select the disappearing feature individually for each person that texts with you, go to the page where you are texting with that person, click on the name on top, and you will see the option to change the amount of time each message from this person will remain live on your device.

On the **App Security,** enable the **Hide Screen in App Switcher** . The next title **Screen Lock** puts us on a pickle because we have talked about not using what you have (face, fingerprints, etc.) to open your technology. In the old days, Signal was allowing the use of a passcode to enter the app. Now, the only choice they provide is your face, as a two-factor verification. This means that when your phone is unlocked, and you tap on the Signal app to use it, you have to open it with your face. In the past, you could enter a passcode to open the app. You know how I feel about this… so I will not tell you what to do, and leave it to your best judgement. One solution, even though it is a pain in the rear end, is to log off the app after using it, and logging back in each time you want to text.

Now, you are ready to send your first text or photo, and/or make a phone call on Signal. For the text, click on the square symbol with a little pencil on the upper right corner of the app. There, you can create a group, find a friend or family by phone number or username. Keep in mind that the other person also needs to have Signal installed.

Did you know that when you take a photo using Signal that photo does not go to the SIM card of your phone? It stays ONLY in the Signal environment until you set it to disappear. Caveat: don't think you have absolute privacy when you Signal photos because the person receiving them can screen shot the photo, and it will have your username or name on top of the screen shot.

You can also make calls using Signal, anywhere in the world, and for free as long as the other person also has Signal installed.

Encrypted Email

If you have an Apple computer, I recommend the tool GPGTools.org. Visit the website, and follow the instructions listed there.

If you have a PC computer, I recommend the Mozilla Thunderbird tool https://www.thunderbird.net/en-US/

Masked Email Addresses

Masking your email addresses is not the same as encrypting the content of the email; however, it is a handy tool offered by Apple devices (see Apple Smartphones and Tablets), and by IronVest (see Figure 1 - IronVest to Store Non-Critical Passwords).

Log into your IronVest account, and from the dashboard, select **Privacy**. This is where you can create a masked email address to use in places where you do not want your real email address to show. If the service where you are using this email address gets hacked, at least your real email address does not end up in the hands of the hacker.

Let's say you want to subscribe to ReadALotMagazine (fictional name for sake of example). When you create an account (on any website), IronVest will offer you to mask your email by showing a popup menu. You agree to mask your email, and IronVest will also create a password for you, if you wish. Now, you have subscribed to this magazine/service with an email address that is not your real email address. The ReadALotMagazine will send you email notifications to the masked email address provided by IronVest which, in turn, will be automatically forwarded to the email address you used to create your IronVest account. When hackers go after ReadALotMagazine, they will steal the masked email address and not your real email address.

This is a great service to safeguard you from the lack of cyber security of third-party services; i.e., places where you do not have any control on how they manage their databases with customer data, etc.

Ghost Emails

As of the writing of this book, this continues to be the most secure form to communicate. In fact, it reminds me of the famous "pizzino" which is a very small paper that the mafia bosses use to write a succinct message and pass it along. No traces left; unless, the messenger is caught with the paper.

The ghost email never navigates through the Internet. It remains floating in no man's land.

How does it work?

You need to create an email account with Gmail, Yahoo or your email provider of choice. You will then share the username and login with the person with whom you want to communicate. DO NOT use your work email address for this. You cannot share your work email credentials.

You now access the email account and write a note in the body of the email BUT YOU NEVER CLICK SEND. You will save the email as draft. You will inform the other party, using another means of comms such as text, that there is a message waiting. The other party will log into the email account using the same username and password you used, go to draft, read the message, delete, and write a reply WITHOUT CLICKING SEND. The only thing you and the other person do is saving the message as draft.

When the message is in the draft, it never travels through the Internet.

How can you get caught?

If you or the other party use that email address to send a message to another person with threatening language, and the other person reports that threat to a law enforcement agency, then your secret email address will be discovered.

If the other person decides to take screen shots of whatever you write on the draft messages, and that person wants to blackmail you or report you to law enforcement, then you get caught.

In simple terms, do not break the law just because you have learned about ghost emails. The perfect crime died in 1996. Now, we have amazing technological tools to trace anything back to the point of origin.

Rules of Engagement

If you are using this to communicate with a confidential informant, the following are important steps to follow to protect you.

1. If you are going to use this method to communicate with an informant, do not use your own technology ever to access this account, and ensure you have the blessing of your bosses in writing. Should the confidential informant decide to go bananas with that email address, you want to have your rear end well-covered.
2. Do not use your personal Wi-Fi to access this email address, for example, when you are at home but using department issued mobile devices. Even though the device might have a VPN, if that account becomes active because the CI has misused it, then you are putting yourself and your family at risk.
3. Always assume the account could have been compromised. In other words, the CI might have been discovered and the person texting is now either under duress or another person.
4. Take screen shots of each incoming draft you read, ensure that time stamp is visible on the screen shot. Do the same for every outgoing draft you write.

If you are using a ghost email because you are having an extramarital affair, the following are important steps to consider:

1. DO NOT use your work Internet connection to access the account.
2. ONLY use your personal devices to access this account. In other words, do not log into this account from your work computer or issued phone.
3. Assume that the other person can take screen shots of everything you write, and that can be used to blackmail you at any time.

In 2012, a director of one of the most important intelligence agencies in the country was having an affair. When he needed to connect his personal mobile device to the Internet, he was too lazy to go to a public place, such a restaurant or coffee house, and too cheap to buy his own Verizon Jet Pack to have his own personal Wi-Fi connection, so he decided to use the Wi-Fi of this very important intelligence agency. Everything was going rosy for him and his lover, until one day, his lover used that account to send a threatening email to another women. What do I tell you that the other woman had a bestie who was a Special Agent at another important federal agency. When the investigators began following IP addresses, and breadcrumbs left behind in those emails, Bingo!! The director having the affair got caught with the hands up to the elbow in the cookie jar.

I could care less what you do with your personal life. However, I care a great deal when your cyber negligence puts all Americans at risk.

CHAPTER 5 – ENCRYPTED STORAGE

You have already discovered one type of storage that you can encrypt with your own password: the WD Passport External Hard Drive.

We have talked about the lack of security of the iCloud, Google Drive, and Microsoft OneDrive. iCloud uses an encryption algorithm of AES-128. In today's cyber environment, this is a bloody joke of security. It is as if you tell me that you secure the front door of your house with a bubble gum so nobody can open it.

Google Drive and Microsoft OneDrive only use one algorithm, AES-256. Even though, this is a step up in security compared to the iCloud, it is not enough to keep your data safe.

For storing data in the cloud, **best encrypted service is Dropbox** (https://www.dropbox.com/). It encrypts data in transit, from your device to the cloud and the cloud to your device, and at rest inside the Dropbox cloud. It uses two different algorithms for encryption. Dropbox offers affordable subscription services for up to 2TB of storage which is usually more than enough for personal use. It also has plans for professionals and businesses.

Once you signed for a Dropbox account, you need to bring the Dropbox icon to your computer, and mobile devices so you can access your files anywhere and anytime. On your browser of choice, type **Download Dropbox for** [Mac or PC – according to what you have], and follow the instructions on the screen. If you have a Mac, you will see the Dropbox icon as shown in Figure 18 - Mac Finder Showing Dropbox Icon on Top.

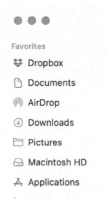

Figure 18 - Mac Finder Showing Dropbox Icon on Top

From this point on, once you have installed your Dropbox app in your computer, you will save all of your documents to your Dropbox where you can create folders, and also encrypt the folder with your own password if you have installed the GPGTools.org or Mozilla Thunderbird explained in Encrypted Email.

If you want to encrypt the folder or file, as shown in Figure 19 - How to Encrypt a Folder, right click on the folder or file. A long pop-up menu shows in the screen. Look at the very bottom, you will see **Services.** Select that and the computer presents you with many choices. If you are doing this on a Mac, you will select OpenPGP: Encrypt File and follow the instructions on the screen.

Figure 19 - How to Encrypt a Folder

On the Dropbox app of your mobile device (which you can download from the Apple Store or Google Play), look at the bottom for the icon **Account**, and select it. On the upper right corner, you will see a wheel, click on it. Select whether you want to **Use cellular data** (this depends on whether you have unlimited data plan). Below that, you will see the title **Passcode lock**. Select **Turn passcode on**, and on the next scree enter a four-digit code (please do not use your birthdate or the last four digits of your SSN or phone).

Keep scrawling down the page, until you see the **Privacy** title. Remember to clear the search history and cache often, and in particular, before you travel.

CHAPTER 6 - VIRTUAL PRIVATE NETWORKS

A Virtual Private Network (VPN) is an encrypted Internet connection between your device and the website you are trying to reach.

Imagine you are in your backyard which has a type of fence that does not give you visual of your neighbor; nevertheless, you both can still carry a conversation through the fence. As you speak, anything you say can be heard and recorded by anyone. This is your Internet connection without a VPN. See the man-in-the-middle intercepting your connection in Figure 20 – Connection without VPN.

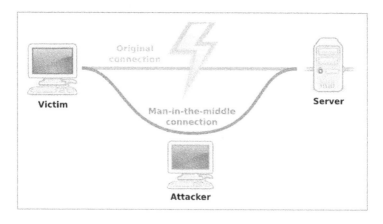

Figure 20 – Connection without VPN

Now, you decide to have private conversations with your neighbor without the risk of being heard by anyone else. You install a PVC pipe through the fence, and your neighbor and you talk through the PVC pipe. This is your connection to the Internet with a VPN. Nobody can intercept the message in the middle.

My favorite VPN service is TunnelBear (https://www.tunnelbear.com/). It is affordable. It works on your computer and mobile devices. It has a great customer service, and it is easy to use.

Why the man-in-the-middle is so dangerous?

This type of attack manipulates information between your device and the website you are visiting. For example, you want to log into the website of your bank account, and the man-in-the-middle attacker will take you to a cloned page of your bank. You enter your username and password, and you get a message saying it is not working. By the time you log into your real bank page, the attacker has stolen all of your beans.

When do I need to use a VPN?

I recommend using it all the time, including when you are connected to a Wi-Fi at home. Most importantly, you must use a VPN every time you are out and about. This includes but are not limited to hotels, restaurants, airport, hospital, your friend's home, etc., etc. The VPN also encapsulates your web searches when you are using cellular data.

Unfortunately, some banking institutions, and services like Amazon.com, do not allow you to use a VPN to log in. The work around is:

- If you are trying to connect a laptop to the Internet, use the hotspot of your mobile device to connect to the Internet. Then, you can visit any website. For example, the Apple Hotspot is encrypted. It uses the ECDH (Curve25519) ephemeral key to secure the connection between users. Mobile hotspots use the robust WPA2 encryption which is difficult to crack.
- If you need to connect to that website with your mobile device, and the website does not like that you are using a VPN, closed all of your apps, log into the Wi-Fi and the website, and then immediately turn your VPN on.

Do VPNs mask my footprint?

The VPN does not hide your searches on a website site. It only hides your IP address to that website. This is one of the reasons you should not use your personal devices to search work related topics. Even though you will be protecting your IP address with a VPN, you are creating a pattern of searches that together can be triangulated to discover your operation, or approximate your location, etc.

For example, imagine that you are driving a vehicle with the Department of Motor Vehicles (DVM) issued license plate (this is equivalent to the IP address of your naked Internet connection, without the VPN). You decide to drive by the house of a person of interest, and you do not want to be identify with that vehicle. Thus, you get a different license plate (VPN gives you a different IP address) that you put on the vehicle thinking that after you are done with the drive-by, you can switch to the original license plate and you will get away with that.

In the vehicle, as well as in the computer, there are many other points of identification that will allow those you are watching to conclude without reasonable doubt that you are the person who did what you did. The VPN masked the IP address but not the content of what you write, or the searches you do when visiting a website.

How about those who break the law while using a VPN? If that person has a VPN on the computer or mobile device, and let's assume the person is committing an Internet crime against the wellbeing of children. That person will have a different IP address which will be difficult to track. However, when that person lands in a website, and searches on how to commit a crime, or looking for specific images, etc., the webmaster will immediately alert the authorities, and with a lot of patience and some search warrants in place, the individual will be discovered.

Can VPNs get hacked?

Yes, the provider of the virtual private network can get hacked and all those IP addresses be released in the open, or the hacker can become man-in-the-middle even if you have the VPN on.

For this reason, use a VPN company that takes cyber security seriously. A VPN company that offers you free VPN is making you the product. In other words, it is somehow selling your information to make money.

How to configure your VPN?

Assuming that you will follow my recommendation, and create an account with TunnelBear, you can expect the following. After installing the software, which you will need to download from its website, you will see the symbol of a honeypot on the upper right corner of your computer. See Figure 21 - TunnelBear Virtual Private Network (VPN).

Figure 21 - TunnelBear Virtual Private Network (VPN)

On the upper left corner, move the slide on the bottom to the right to turn it green. On the image above, it is gray meaning it is off. You want to have that green.

The first choice **Fastest** will connect you to the first country of TunnelBear preference in relationship to your location to give you the fastest connection. I have stated before that you always want to be in control of what you use. Therefore, it is better if you select the **United States** option, and from there you select any city of your preference.

You can play with pretending to be in different countries to access content that might not be available in your own country. For example, I love to listen to podcasts in the five languages I speak. Therefore, I select France as my VPN location so I can see on the Apple Store many options of Podcasts I can subscribe to.

When you are looking at information related to your case, you can also select a different country to throw the webmaster of that website in a different direction. Let's say that you are looking at a mafia organization in New York, set your VPN to Italy. Two things will happen: your search engine will show you content that you might not have seen if you would have just used the USA location, and if you find some blog of interest, the webmaster will not suspect that anyone in the USA is looking at that data.

CHAPTER 7 - TWO-FACTOR AUTHENTICATION

Today, practically all services offer a form of two-step authentication, also known as two-factor authentication (2FA). This means that in order to access any of your accounts, you need to provide username and password first, then you will receive a text, or email, or phone call, or instructions to open an authentication app to retrieve an additional number that you need to input to finally access your account.

Social media accounts, banks, email, health organization, and many more offer this essential security feature. Some give you the option to download the Google Authenticator app instead of using your phone number and/or email. You can find this app in the Apple Store or Google play. The app issues random numbers. When you want to sign for a service for which you have selected the Google Authenticator as your two-factor authentication (2FA), you will need to open the Google Authenticator app on your phone, and enter on the account you are trying to access the number you see on the screen of the Google Authenticator app.

Note that Google Authenticator allows you to add it on to your browser, as well.

Figure 22 - Google Authenticator

This is an essential cyber defense feature.

CHAPTER 8 - TRAVELING

Airports and hotels are the most common hunting grounds to access your data, hack you, phish you, and social engineer you. If you have followed all the recommendations above, you have a pretty secure device from the technical point of view. You have also learned some behavior modifications that you must implement in your daily routine to ensure that your cyber perimeter is always solid.

While traveling, behavior is the most important aspect of your cyber security. The how and where you use your phone, along with what information to access and when to access it will assist you in keeping hackers away from your data.

Before departure

- Backup phones to laptop or desktop

- Backup laptop or desktop to external hard drive

- Put this external hard drive on a safe in your home

- Make a note of serial numbers of all devices your transport, and upload that file (encrypted) to the Dropbox

- Ensure your VPN subscription is up to date and that you have the VPN turned on your mobile devices, and laptop (when you start using it)

- Pack the cables you will need to charge your devices using an electric outlet (or cigarette lighter) and not the USB chargers at the airports or rental cars.

- Ensure you have encrypted your Android mobile devices, and your laptop (Apple or PC)

- Take a photo of your passport, driver's license, car insurance, and medical insurance card, upload them to the Dropbox and encrypt that folder. Remember you will be able to access the Dropbox from anywhere and anytime in case your documents get stolen.

- When you travel abroad, have handy the address and phone numbers for the American Embassy/Consulate.

- Carry all important files on the Dropbox. Ensure you have added a passcode to the app as explained in CHAPTER 5 – ENCRYPTED STORAGE.

- Print driving directions of your destination. Did you know that in every airport in the world, your data gets sucked out of your phone within 10 miles of the airport? If you are traveling to a foreign country, you will carry your technology in a Faraday case (see below). Thus, when you reach your destination, instead of the tempting behavior of pulling your phone to call an Uber or Lyft, use the printed direction of where you want to go. Then, get either the metro, bus or an airport taxi. Once you have past the 10-mile mark, you can open your phone. I always like to engage Waze to ensure the driver is not giving me the round around, and I tell the driver that I want to follow the Waze instructions to the T. Remember that in the majority of countries, airport taxis are regulated and safer than Uber and Lyft.

- Purchase a faraday bag, and put your technology inside it. The following are marks and models I recommend:

  - SLNT https://slnt.com/

  - ConcealShield - https://defendershield.com/concealshield?ref=emfa

  - Mission Darkness 15L Dry Shield Faraday Tote

- Purchase a camera detector with GPS tracker detector for car. I recommend this one or similar functionality https://amzn.to/4cJ9sQG Use to sweep hotel rooms and rental homes.

- •

- •   *Figure 23 - Camera / GPS Detector https://amzn.to/4cJ9sQG*

Upon Arriving at the Airport

Print your boarding pass at any of the stations provided at the airport, if you did not do this at home (my preferred choice). Do not use your phone to check-in. The minute you put that phone in the airline scan, your data gets sucked.

You will not be able to use the VPN when you try to connect to the airplane Wi-Fi, so bring a paper book and use the time in the air to write by hand or read the old fashion way. Most airplanes these days offer you their own entertainment center.

If you really need to work on your computer, buy a screen that protects it from the curious eyes of those sitting around you, and work off-line (not connected to the Wi-Fi). You will not be able to use your mobile Hotspot once you are up in the air.

At the airport, do not use the Wi-Fi offered to you there. If you need to use your laptop, use the Hotspot of your mobile device.

At the hotel or wherever you will sleep while traveling

Ensure all apps in the device you want to connect to the Internet are closed.

Ensure your VPN is on.

Now, connect to the hotel Wi-Fi. Some hotels are tricky sneaky, and they do not allow you to connect to the Wi-Fi with the VPN on. You can momentarily turn it off, connect to the hotel Wi-Fi and then engage the VPN. Once you are with VPN running, you can start opening websites and apps.

When you check out, take the electronic key cards with you. Those cards contain all of your data that the hotel collected from you. Shred them when you get home.

Public Spaces in Foreign Countries

If you are visiting a country outside the U.S.A., keep in mind that the thievery of mobile phones is high. For example, in Barcelona, Spain, the thieves operate in groups of three or four. One keeps an eye on where you carry your phone and how alert you are of your environment. That person informs the position of your phone to the one who will snatch it, and another will bump on you at the same time, and the snatcher passes the phone to a fourth person who you have not seen so you can't even chase if you wanted. In Buenos Aires, Argentina, the problem is the same. On the other hand, in Italy, everybody walks with their phones in hand using the navigator to go from one historical mark to the other without having problems.

If you happen to visit a country where phone thievery is high, carry the phone on front pockets, do not pull it out in public transportation, and go inside a bank or business to conspicuously check your phone.

Renting a car

Do not connect your phone to the car Bluetooth or USB. Use the cigarette lighter USB adapter to charge your phone. Make sure you have bought all the cables needed for your type of devices.

CHAPTER 9 – SURFING THE WEB UNDETECTED

After Alphabet, Inc. (owner of Google search engine) announced that the incognito mode of their browser was actually a joke because they were tracking everything, the suggestion of surfing the web undetected might sound like an oxymoron.

Nevertheless, there are ways and browsers that will allow you to minimize the data you disclose while navigating the Internet.

The following are browsers that I use, such as DuckDuckGo, and two of the most used: Google and Safari. If you use Mozilla Firefox, a browser that I stopped trusting in 2015, go to the settings and configure it following the knowledge you are about to learn from configuring Google Chrome below. I cannot describe every browser in the marketplace so I decided to limit the conversation to my favorite, and a few well-known and used.

Make sure you have your VPN on and location services off.

Google Chrome

When you are using this browser, and as per Alphabet, Inc. declaration, the only difference between open and incognito mode is that the incognito mode protects you against the curious eyes of other members of your household. For example, if you are looking for something on the Internet at home and you do not want anyone else to find out, you use the incognito screen, and once you close it, it is supposed to take away your search history. The reality is that it does not. You need to manually remove search history from every browser you use.

How to configure your Google Chrome:

Although this configuration will not give you a 100% privacy protection, it will at least cut some of the spill. Nevertheless, remember that for Alphabet, Inc./Google, you are the product.

1. Open a Google Chrome page. Ensure you are not sign in to your Google account if you have one. You do not need to sign in to your account to surf the web.
2. Click on the three vertical dots that you will find on the upper right corner of the Google screen, and select **Passwords and Autofill**. Turn that feature off because you are now saving your passwords with IronVest which is a better platform. On the left panel of the **Password and Autofill** window, you see **Settings.** Click on it and the right panel shows you that IronVest is managing your passwords. On that same screen, turn off **Sign in automatically**. DO NOT import your passwords here.
3. Click again on the three vertical dots on the upper right corner of the Google screen, and select **History**. If you have never cleared your browsing history, you will see an extensive collection of websites. On the left panel, click on **Delete browsing history**, and on the window that pops up, select the **Advanced** tab and select all the options there. On the **Time Rage** select **All time**
4. When you are done clearing your browsing history, Google shows you this screen (Figure 24 - Google Settings)

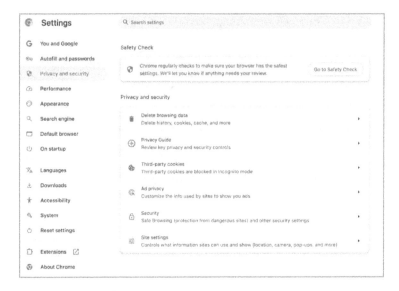

Figure 24 - Google Settings

5. Click on **Third-party cookies** and **Block third-party cookies in incognito mode.** Turn on **Send a "Do not track" request…**

6. On the left panel, select the title **On startup** and mark **Open the New Tab page**.

7. On the left panel, select **Downloads** and enable both features: **Ask where to save…** and **Show download when they're done**.

8. On the left panel, select **Extensions**. On the left panel of that page, you see **Discover more extensions…** and a link to enter the Google store. Click on that, and install the following extensions:
    a. AdBlock for YouTube
    b. AdBlock Plus
    c. Disconnect
    d. Google Analytics OptOut
    e. Ghostery
    f. Privacy Badger
    g. HTTPS Somewhere
    h. Keyboard Privacy

Remember that you have installed the IronVest extension which provides you with tracker blockers as well. See Figure 25 - Iron Vest Protection Against Tracking

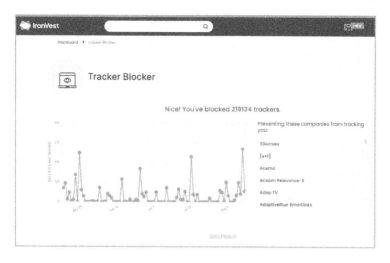

Figure 25 - Iron Vest Protection Against Tracking

Safari

Apple, Inc. owns this browser. For everything you search in Safari, you are the product. Apple, Inc. needs to make money out of your curiosity, the same way that Alphabet, Inc., and other with the exception of DuckDuckGo.

With the browser open, on the upper left corner of your computer, click on the Safari word and select **Preferences.** See Figure 26 - Safari Preferences.

Figure 26 - Safari Preferences

From the **General** tab, the first choice is cheap macaroni because you can either show all the windows from the last session or All non-private windows… So make sure that you select **Empty Page** on the next two options from that window. On the **Remove history items**, select **After one day.** On the **File Download location**, select **Ask for each download**. On the **Remove download list items**, you can mark **After on day** if you tend to leave the browser open overnight or **When Safari quits** if you have the discipline to close the browser when you are not using it.

From the top of the **Preferences** window, select the tab **Security** and mark both options.

From the top, select the tab **Privacy** and mark **Website tracking, Hide IP address**, and **Web advertising**.

Note that if you mark **Block all the cookies** many websites will not work. So since the websites are required to present you with the option to decline cookies, you can set your privacy there.

On the main window, select the tab **Websites**. On the left panel that shows up after you select the tab websites, select **Camera** and at the bottom of the right panel, select **When visiting other websites:** Ask. Do the same for **Microphone, Screen Sharing**, **Location**, and **Downloads**. On the last option, on the left panel, **Pop-up Windows** select **Block and Notify**.

DuckDuckGo

This is by far my favorite browser. I hope you will give it a try. Visit duckduckgo.com and download the app on your computer. You can also install it on your mobile devices.

Why is DuckDuckgo better than Google, Safari, Mozilla Firefox, etc.? Because DuckDuckGo doesn't track the websites your visit, and it does not store user data. The best part is that it uses encrypted connections to protect your searches from those who are eager to snoop on what you are looking for online. DuckDuckGo shows users how privately they're surfing the web and grades websites from A–F based on their privacy.

The results you obtain from searching in DuckDuckgo do not have bias in terms of popularity or what other web browsers, like Google, do that push on to you what they think you will like. This practice of Google and others alike create a silo of knowledge because those search engines show you what they think you might want to read. However, you might find something else that you want to read that was not shown to you by the search engine because Google made a decision for you, rather than you deciding on what you want to see.

This browser is practically a plug and play. You can visit the **Settings** page and make selections according to your preferences.

CHAPTER 10 – SOCIAL MEDIA

Social media apps are the perfect environment for social engineering you, catfishing you, and exhorting money if you do not diligently research to whom you are donating to. This is particularly common during natural disasters.

I could write a whole separate book about this topic in terms of the damage it has done to children, some adults with addiction issues, relationships, etc. It has also helped business with advertising, and law enforcement with open-source information intelligence.

I can compare it with the ethanol in wine and other alcoholic beverages: you know ethanol is super toxic to your body; however, you decide that one glass a day will not kill you right away. It will cause damage in the long term but you will live many years enjoying it. No matter how many pages I write about both of this topic, I do not think I will make a dent on your behavior modification towards them: you will continue scrolling through the Instagram reels with a glass of wine in your hands.

Therefore, let's focus on the cyber defense aspect of your social media accounts. All are run by companies who offer you to create accounts for free because you are the product of those companies. In other words, all the information you spill over these accounts serves the marketing purposes of companies like Meta (Facebook and Instagram), X, Pinterest, etc. This problem is compounded when you have the location services On and the Bluetooth On all the time.

There is a lot of chatter and concern about Facebook spying on cellphones through the microphone. The company has vehemently denied it. So, how do they know when you need cold medication? Because of your postings online, and your location services on when you are walking along the store's aisles.

For example, you post on any social media that you think you are coming down with a cold, and several hours later, you open your Facebook app and Bingo! Facebook is offering you a discount coupon for a pharmacy that has that medication at half price. Facebook collects data from your movements around the web (VPN is a must at all times, location services OFF), and in the physical world when you are at the market and with your location services on, Facebook can see what aisles you are stopping by and for how long. At the market, you use your phone number to get points for your purchase. A third-party associated with the market collects that data and sells that data to Facebook. This third-party also sells that data to the pharmaceutical companies that sell cold medication.

DO NOT use your personal device to create a fake account to monitor any person or organization related to your work. You need to ask your department for a work-issued mobile device, or limit the creation and use of that account to your work computer.

If you need assistance with creating a solid strategy for communicating a crisis or a high-profile incident, I highly recommend your reaching out to Julie Parker Communications (https://julieparkerco.com/) who among its experts has Chief of Police (Ret.) Christopher Mannino.

Behavior Modification: 1) Turn location services OFF on your mobile devices at all times; except when you are in your car and need to use your navigation app to reach your destination; and 2) Use a VPN on your mobile device at all time because it protects your IP address not only when you use a Wi-Fi connection, but also when you are on cellular data.

Now, I have an ethical question for you to ponder upon regarding photos posted in social media. If you are a parent, you are the advocate for the safety of your children. My question is: **what gives you the right to plaster the Internet with their photos when they are below the age of consent?**

Social Engineering

The Oxford Dictionary defines social engineering in the information security field as the utilization of deception to manipulate individuals into divulging personal or confidential information with the purpose of using it for fraudulent purposes.

Where can social engineering occur?

In the physical domain such as your workplace, phone, your garbage when you put the trash out in the street. In the virtual domain, you can be social engineered in social media platforms (LinkedIn being the most common for this purpose), texting, and/or sending you an email with an infected link for you to click on (phishing).

The psychological tools used by social engineers are persuasion, impersonation (telling you they are an employee of a federal law enforcement agency), conformity (you are too lazy to research the email or text, or LinkedIn invitation), diffusion of responsibility (I will get your ass fired if you do not comply), and the old fashion friendliness (the person waiting in the reception area making conversation with the receptionist/secretary and inquiring about one of the executives of the company). The examples in between parenthesis are just a few of the many ways social engineers will try to navigate to obtain the desired information. To learn more about this, and to assist you in educating your children, visit https://www.social-engineer.org/

As of the writing of this book, these are the most common social engineering scams you might encounter, and they are not limited to the list below:

- Phishing: You receive an email, text or post in social media with convincing information that you must click on a link or else… that link has malware and it will infect your device, or you will end up entering your credit card information in the crook's website.
- Vishing: Same as above but done over the phone.
- Smishing: Phishing done over text.
- Spear phishing: It is a personalized form of phishing. Let's say you won the lottery, and the newspaper did an article on your winning. You could be the victim of spear phishing.
- Whaling: It is a personalized phishing that includes personal communication. The hacker conducts extensive research, and this type of attack is usually successful.
- Watering hole attacks, as described on page 15.
- Quid pro quo: The attacker asks the victim for something in

exchange. For example, you send me $600 so I can process a check for you in the amount of $60,000.

- Tech support, rebate and/or legal scams: Probably you have received a phone call, text or email about your technology not working properly, money you have in a refund account that has not been claimed, etc., etc. Unless you have called a tech support or repairing service, do not allow anyone to touch your Internet connection just because they called you.

- Scareware: You visit an infected website, and suddenly a window in red color pops up saying that your computer has been infected. Just close the website, and all that goes away.

- Impersonating authority: The attacker impersonates someone the victim knows as a manager, CEO or colleague.

In all the attacks above, there is a common denominator: the use of fear and urgency to pressure you to take the action the attacker wants you to do.

Solutions:

1. DO NOT click on links no matter who send them to you… boss, family member, etc. because you do not know whether the computer of the sender has been compromised (infected) by the attacker. Go directly to the website. For example, if your banking institution or your spouse says that the bank account balance is low, and the email has a link to the bank account, use your browser to enter manually the website address of your banking institution. DO NOT click on the link.

2. You get a phone call, and the caller tells you that it is from bank, or medical institution, or Internal Revenue Service, or whatever; and the caller asks you for personally identifiable information such as your social security number, date of birth, etc., or even any question for that matter, you will politely tell the caller that you will call back the institution yourself. DO NOT use the number that the caller will give you. Use the number that you always use to reach that institution.

3. Stop sending money to those who convince you that they have a large check to cash but they need an advance in good faith that you will then return their money, etc. This type of fraud is usually perpetrated by Nigerians. It is also known as the 419 fraud when you receive a letter. Now, with the advantage of the Internet, even the crooks have

modernized their techniques so they are serving you the scam via your electronic devices. According to the FBI, in 2023, older Americans lost $3.4 billion dollars![17] If you believe you have been a victim of a scam in which you have lost money, please visit ic3.gov to report the crime to the FBI.

4. You would rather have to defend your position for having done due diligence in denying a caller access than getting fired for giving access to the crown jewels of the organization. When someone threatens you with getting you fired on the phone, just hang up, and report the incident to your security department.

5. In LinkedIn, even though there are many forms to use that platform to social engineer you, you can set your connections to be visible only to you. This will give you a little bit of protection to you and your connections. See Recommendations for the LinkedIn Account.

Recommendations for the LinkedIn Account

If you are still on the force, there is no need for you to spill all the details of every op you have taken part of. Most importantly, DO NOT put the level of clearance you hold. If you are thinking about leaving the force, and using LinkedIn to find you a job with a private company, you can put details on a resume or cover letter that you send individually to each company who could be a potential employer.

The manipulation of the settings is easier done from your computer. Click on your photo and select **Settings and Privacy**. On the new screen, from the left panel, select **Account Preferences**. On the right panel look for **Personal demographic information** and do not add anything here, and if you have added delete it. Keep scrolling down the page till you see **People also viewed**, and mark if **Off**.

On the left panel, select **Sign & Security**. On the right panel, ensure you select **On** for **Two-step verification**.

On the left panel, select **Visibility**. On the right-hand panel, turn **Profile viewing options** to **Private mode** so nobody can see that you have looked

---

[17] https://www.ic3.gov/Media/PDF/AnnualReport/2023_IC3ElderFraudReport.pdf accessed on August 2024.

at their profile. On the second title, **Page visit visibility** also turn it **Off**.

We are still on the right panel of the **Visibility** section, and you are looking at **Who can see or download your email address**. Select **Only visible to me** or **1ˢᵗ Degree connections.** At the bottom of that page, marked **Off** the option **Allow connection to export emails**.

Again, from the **Visibility** section, and on the right-hand panel, look for the title **Connections** and mark it **Off**. This way, others cannot see who you are connected to and this will help curtail some of the social engineering scams. Then, look for **Profile discovery and visibility** and turn it **Off**. For **Profile discovery using email address** select **1ˢᵗ degree connections**, and for **Profile discovery using phone number** select **Nobody**.

From the left-hand panel, select **Data Privacy** and clear your search history. This is something that I recommend doing periodically. On the title **Social, economic, and workplace research** turn it **Off**.

On the left-hand panel, select **Advertising Data**. On the right-hand panel, for the title **Connections, Companies you follow**, and **Groups** turn them **Off**. You will start seeing a lot of less advertising on your LinkedIn feed. Still on the right-hand panel, look for **Activity and inferred data** and turn **Off** all of those options. Finally, for the last title on the right-hand panel, **Third-party data** turn them all **Off**.

I highly recommend that you periodically visit the LinkedIn settings page because Microsoft (who owns LinkedIn) often adds features that infringe in your privacy. When Microsoft adds a feature, it is turned on by default.

Before you accept a LinkedIn invitation

You want to connect with individuals who will bring value to you. For example, I never accept invitations that do not have a message from the person telling me why they want to connect. I reply asking for the reason of the invite, without accepting the invitation. I want to know why that person wants to enter my network or connect with me. If the answer is because we have connections in common, I do not accept it. This person is a troller and is looking to add connections to exploit them in some form or another.

Look at the list of companies and titles the person has worked for. Do they seem real to you or do they look like Eddy Logan (note that this profile is no longer available in LinkedIn; however, it was an active profile in or around 2014), see Figure 27 - LinkedIn Profile circa 2014.

Figure 27 - LinkedIn Profile circa 2014

From the photo, you see the logos for the FBI and CIA. They keep secrets indeed but not in the same closet. On his list of career accomplishments, he claimed to be the Chief Advisor for the White House in 2013, and at the same time a landscaper in New York. I could go on and on but I think you get the gist of doing due diligence before accepting an invitation.

Books Recommendations

For the topic of social engineering, and one of the most dangerous underground groups in the Internet, I recommend reading the books of the late Kevin D. Mitnick, and Parmy Olson's *We are anonymous*.

CHAPTER 11 – FREEZING YOUR CREDIT

In spite all the security measures recommended in the previous chapters, you cannot control how third parties handle your data and credentials such as social security number, maiden names, etc.

Moreover, there are many databases that aggregate your data such as Spokeo, Truthfinder, etc. Those databases contain the needed information to get credit cards and other transactions on your name unbeknown to you.

Freezing your credit report is one of the most efficient ways to block an unscrupulous individual from opening a credit line with your data. You will need to visit the website of the three reporting agencies, and follow their instructions.

1) Equifax: https://www.equifax.com/personal/credit-report-services/credit-freeze/
2) Transunion: https://www.transunion.com/credit-freeze
3) Experian:
   https://www.experian.com/freeze/center.html

When you need to open a new credit card or purchase a vehicle, house, etc., you will need to unfreeze the line for 24 hours, and then freeze it again.

EPILOGUE

It is an illusion to think that you can have 100% security guaranteed in the physical and cyber domains. You have to accept a degree of risk. Ideally, you will aim for a degree of risk that it is away from the 100%. For example, a 10% level of risk is a good one. You can be in control of 90% of most situations; however, there is a 10% for which you have zero control. In the cyber domain, that encompasses the desire of companies to safeguard your data, someone stealing your devices, etc.

The goal of this book is to help you reach that low level of risk by using a combination of technology and behavior modification. Now, it is up to you to accept my advice line by line or pick and choose.

I strongly believe that when each individual takes responsibility to harden the cyber perimeter, the cyber security of the nation becomes stronger against domestic and international malicious actors who are making billions of dollars from theft of data, and ransomware demands.

When your credit card number is stolen online, and it gets charged for things, you call the credit card company who will refund you the money back to your account. Where do you think this money comes from? The credit card does not call Vladimir from the Eurasian Cyber Mafia and ask for the money back. The money comes from the U.S. Treasury Department. Each year, billions of dollars end up in the hands of these criminals. You have the power to help stop that.

When you are cyber responsible, you are showing your patriotism. Cyber security is each one of us responsibility. I urge you to do your part.

Thank you for reading!

ACKNOWLEDGMENT

Many thanks to all who supported me throughout my career. Specials thanks to the late U.S. Navy SEAL Thomas Maher who was instrumental in bringing my program to the Teams; and to retired Police Chief Christopher Mannino who encouraged me to create a book out of my cyber defense course.

ABOUT THE AUTHOR

Cecilia Anastos holds a Master's Degree in Strategic Intelligence with specialty in Middle East Issues, a Graduate Certificate in Cybercrime, a B.A. in Criminal Justice w/sp in Psychology, and a Dog Trainer degree from the Animal Behavioral College.

Fluent in five languages, she is a pioneer in the utilization of digitized open source and publicly available information to create actionable intelligence, and in the reduction of digital signatures in the cyberspace domain. She designed the first cyber defense course of instruction for the US Navy SEALs where she taught for many years. Ms. Anastos also taught this course in many police departments, and the private sector. Between 2011-2012, she was a guest instructor at the FBI National Academy – Quantico, VA.

In 2016, Ms. Anastos was recognized as one of the most influential leaders in the field of cybersecurity by the San Diego Business Journal's SDBJ500.

Other books by the author:
After the Walk – The Amazing Places the Mind Goes (2022)
Thinking with Rhythm (2023)
Cyber Defense for Women (2024)
Cyber Defense for Executives and Board Members (2024)

www.ingramcontent.com/pod-product-compliance
Lightning Source LLC
LaVergne TN
LVHW092030060326
832903LV00058B/497